SANDER'S STUDY

A SON'S STORY

Chris Vanocur
May, 2023

CHRIS VANOCUR

ISBN: 979-8-9854232-0-4 (paperback)
ISBN: 979-8-9854232-1-1 (ebook)

The front cover photograph was taken by Cecil Stoughton in his official capacity as the White House photographer. The portrait of Sander Vanocur on the back cover was drawn by Barnaby Conrad (Courtesy of Virginia Vanocur).

To My Parents,
Who Filled Our House with Books
And Love for the Written Word.

CONTENTS

PROLOGUE

SANDER'S SON.

This is who I have been, who I am, and who I will always be.

I'm the younger of Sander Vanocur's two sons. My father was best known as a star political reporter for NBC News. His distinctive name was familiar to and respected by viewers all over the country. In the 1960s, his heyday, he reported on John and Robert Kennedy, the Vietnam War, the civil rights movement, and Dr. Martin Luther King Jr. Dad not only covered them all but did so with distinction. In fact, he would become as popular and recognizable as the network news anchors themselves.

Journalism was the family business I was born into. It was clearly not a typical upbringing. My privileged childhood was filled with famous newsmakers, lawmakers, and various Hollywood celebrities. I was educated at one of the nation's premier private schools, one also attended by the children of presidents. In a related coincidence, my biology lab partner was a student by the name of Dan Rather Jr.

But the many early blessings bestowed upon me were tempered by a fair amount of turbulence. Assassinations, political vendettas, and family upheaval were also part of my childhood. These rough patches served to upend me when I was young and would continue to haunt my father and me for decades.

Despite this turmoil, though, my father's success and gravitational pull proved to be irresistible. I too became a TV political reporter. Although I wasn't nearly as well known or capable as my father, I did manage to make a decent living at it for more than three decades. I even broke a big national and international story, thus burnishing my own journalistic bona fides.

But by late 2015, I had soured on TV news. I retired in my mid-fifties and, in so doing, assumed my reporting days were behind me. I was mistaken. Little did I realize I still had one more big assignment ahead of me. Without warning, I was handed the story of a lifetime. Actually, it was the story of two lifetimes. It was the story of my father and me.

In the late winter, my stepmother asked for a favor. She wanted me to organize and clean out my father's study. Her specific instructions were to keep what was important and donate or throw out the rest. Normally, Dad would have taken care of it himself, but he was in his mid-eighties and not doing well. Age had finally caught up with him. He simply was no longer up to the task.

Luckily, the timing was perfect for me. I was very much in a transitional phase. While I was relieved to have left TV behind, I was uncertain about what to do next. Repaying my father's affection and support by helping him declutter his memorabilia was the least I could do. And I was also curious about what paternal secrets might lie in his study.

My father and I loved each other unconditionally, but we didn't verbalize it well or express it often. Instead of warm and lengthy embraces, mostly we had formal handshakes. Instead of actually telling my dad how much he meant to me or vice versa, we assumed it was a given and left it unsaid. Thus, in his study, I sought both knowledge and redemption. I hoped what I would find there would help me better understand my father and, in turn, shed new light on our kinship. I feared Dad didn't have much time left and this might be my last chance to draw closer to him.

Fortunately, Dad's final study proved to be a welcoming and picturesque one. It was located in Montecito, California, a tony neighbor of Santa Barbara. His study was in a guest cottage behind the house, just a short walk up the driveway. But the slightly steep ascent was always worth it. At the top, one was rewarded with a beautiful view of both the mountains and the Pacific Ocean.

Over the years, my father's studies were shrines to me. Mystical sorts of places, full of grandeur and wonder. It was in these sacred and sometimes intimidating sanctuaries that my father would write his TV stories, his newspaper and magazine articles, and his many speeches. As a shy, introspective child, I would sometimes sneak into his study when my parents were out of the house. I would sit at his desk awestruck, pretending that his old-school typewriter, his cluttered papers, and aromatic pipes actually belonged to me.

But I soon discovered that the task of tidying up Dad's Montecito study wasn't quite so idyllic as those childhood memories. This new assignment required quite a bit of work. My job entailed methodically sifting through nine decades of my father's career and life. When I agreed to do this, I had no idea what I was getting into. Turns out, Dad kept a lot of stuff. And when I say a lot, I mean everything. I don't think the man ever threw anything away. Imagine, for example, my surprise when I found his car insurance policy from the 1960s (and my amusement when I saw how affordable it was back then).

But this avalanche of paperwork ultimately proved fruitful. It gave me a much more complete picture of my father. I was finally able to see his evolution from a brilliant student to a supernova of a network news star. The documents in his study provided a roadmap to his life. They highlighted his triumphs, his profound defeats, and his phoenix-like rise from those setbacks.

Over the course of several long weeks, I unearthed a treasure trove of personal and political gems. There was the award-winning college speech that first showed his immense promise. Also, a letter to the editor that would dramatically change his life. Equally intriguing were his TV and radio scripts. Dad referred to these news dispatches—as well as those of other journalists—as, "The first rough draft of history." My father's news stories poignantly told the history of America in the second half of the twentieth century. They also hinted at his role in shaping some of these crucial and historic events.

In addition, there were scores of pictures Dad had accumulated over the years. I found myself transfixed by photographs of my father with presidents, leading political figures, civil rights leaders, and even images of him attending chic parties with the powerful and well-to-do. I was also greatly moved by the family photos I came across, some of which I had never seen. Others had been hidden away for decades. There were long-forgotten images of my parents, my brother, and me, young and heavily jowled. These photos immediately reminded me of the joy our family often shared. But some also jogged sorrowful memories of tougher times.

Living in our modern era of impersonal emails and disposable texts, I found myself especially enchanted by Dad's old letters, both the ones he sent and those he received. Some were handwritten, others typed using antiquated machines. There was correspondence from famous politicians, first ladies, notable artists, and even other reporters.

I was especially drawn to my father's exchange of letters with one of his closest friends, Russell Baker. Baker was an immensely gifted and wise columnist for the *New York Times*. Going through Baker's lengthy and humorous handwritten notes to my father, I was reminded of something the columnist once observed. In his delightful and Pulitzer Prize-winning two-part autobiography, Baker wrote about the power of words to take us places. Words took Baker from rural Virginia to New York City and the top echelon of his craft.[1] Words also took my father on an equally remarkable journey. Born in the Depression era, Dad rose to become one of the biggest and most successful names in TV news.

As I plunged deeper into my father's records, my own reporting instincts began to kick in. Several times in my career, I've gotten unusually strong and intuitive feelings about certain people or events. For reasons still unclear, these intuitive moments would suddenly jolt me, fiercely focusing my attention on these individuals or episodes and refusing to let go. I've even gone so far as to refer to these unexpected jolts as my "Spider-Senses."

1. Baker, *The Good Times*.

While Spider-Man's senses tingled when danger was near, my Spider-Senses tingled when I stumbled upon a big story.

This is what happened while combing through my father's study. Looking at all his bygone papers, photographs, and remnants of his life and career, I realized there was a significant tale to be told. It was the story of Dad's remarkable career, the renowned people he crossed paths with, and the historical scenes he witnessed. He had lived a rare life and had stories few could tell.

The difficulty, though, lay in exactly how to tell Dad's story. Initially, I thought it would be a straightforward all-American biography, about how one man's hard work and gumption was ultimately rewarded with riches and fame. But as I pored over my father's papers, a different story also emerged. It was not one I had planned on telling, but I kept coming back to it. Specifically, I was gobsmacked by how closely my own life mirrored his. Where we went to school, what we did for a living, how we talked, how we looked, how we thought. I was Sander's son through and through. I realized to properly tell his story, parts of mine would also have to seep in.

Which is not to say, however, that I didn't have some qualms writing about my father, about me, and about our relationship. One of Dad's cardinal rules of journalism was never to make yourself the story. This was nonnegotiable. You simply did not write or talk about yourself in your stories. Period. No discussion. To do so would be exceedingly vainglorious. Or, in our case, Vanglorious.

Luckily, I also inherited Dad's fierce independent streak. Just because I wasn't supposed to make myself part of the story didn't mean I wouldn't. If I was going to be the chosen son to write his biography, I had to do it my way. This meant writing candidly about both of us. Not only would I be required to write about our triumphs but also our demons, our depression, and our self-destructive tendencies.

Fortunately, my father's study showed me the way forward. The papers

I found squirreled away there illuminated what had been most important to him. These vital episodes of his life ultimately became the individual chapters of this book. Intentionally or not, Dad had left me a blueprint on what to focus on and how to tie all these elements together. I was on a voyage of discovery, and his study served as my trusted guide, my North Star.

As I began to put all this down on paper, I recalled my father's oft-repeated advice about storytelling, "Tell them what you're going to tell them. Tell them. And then tell them what you've told them."

As always, these were wise words from Sander to his son.

Chapter One

A State of Mind

I SCREWED UP.

Within minutes of starting to organize Dad's study, I got rid of something I shouldn't have.

Feeling overwhelmed as I stared at ninety years' worth of documents, I quickly grew impatient. Dad had accumulated so much stuff in his nine decades, I honestly didn't know how I was going to get through it all. So, in my haste to declutter, I mistakenly threw away an important document.

In my defense, it didn't initially appear to be all that noteworthy. It was nothing more than a stapled group of faded papers, maybe a half dozen pages in all. The title on the cover said, "A State of Mind." Below that were three smaller lines:

Sander Vanocur
Northwestern University
1949

I quickly and haphazardly flipped through the pages. I incorrectly concluded it was simply one of many papers he had written in college. As far as I could tell, it had something to do with our relationship with Russia. Deeming it inconsequential, I tossed it without care into the garbage bin.

It wasn't until the next day that I realized the huge mistake I'd made. I was going through a folder of some of Dad's early press clippings and I saw a *Daily Northwestern* article from February 16, 1949. The headline read, "Vanocur Wins First in 72nd Annual Kirk Oratorical Contest." This got my attention. Could this have been Dad's first brush with fame? Intrigued, I read on.

But my mood abruptly changed when I got to the second line of the story. That's when I started freaking out.

The second sentence began, "Vanocur, in his speech, 'A State of Mind…'"[2] Horror-stricken, I stopped reading. My blunder had just been revealed. I hadn't just thrown away one of Dad's college papers; I had literally trashed one of his earliest success stories. My father had just turned twenty-one and had won a very prestigious award for his oratory skills.

But the next press clipping made my stomach turn even more. This time it was a *Daily Northwestern* article from Tuesday, May 10, 1949. This headline proclaimed, "Vanocur Wins Northern Speech Meet."[3] Winning the Kirk Oratorical made my father eligible for the 59th annual Northern Oratorical League contest. In this prestigious tournament, Dad competed against students from Iowa, Minnesota, Michigan, and Wisconsin. And, of course, he won this second contest by giving the "State of Mind" speech.

I was crestfallen. Within minutes of starting to go through Dad's papers, I had mistakenly tossed away a revealing and not insignificant part of his life's story.

One of my decidedly unhelpful yet persistent personality traits is to obsess over my mistakes, even the small ones. While throwing away an award-winning speech clearly wasn't a smart thing to do, it also wasn't exactly the end of the world. But, as is my wont, I internalized it and let it eat away at me. I tossed and turned at night, mentally punishing myself for a costly unforced error. I even ridiculously worried I wouldn't be able to write this book without that speech.

Luckily, though, Dad was a hoarder. Several days later, I was immensely relieved to discover another copy of "A State of Mind." In fact, I ended up finding several copies of this speech in his study. Not for the first—or

2. *Daily Northwestern*, "Vanocur Wins First."
3. *Daily Northwestern*, "Vanocur Wins Northern Speech Meet."

last—time, Dad had come to my rescue. He was smart enough to have made sure his speech would be preserved for posterity.

Having been given a second chance, I pored over his award-winning address slowly and carefully. It readily became apparent why Dad had won those speaking contests. It was an impressive, tightly written, and well-reasoned piece of work. The fact that he was just twenty-one years old makes it even more remarkable.

The first line of the speech immediately hooks you: "I received a letter last December that I was afraid to open." It was a clever way to start. My father instantly grabbed the audience's attention by personalizing his story.

Dad also hinted at a bit of mystery, a shrouded secret. What could possibly be in a letter that would scare such a smart and confident young man? Dad continued this mysterious tease in the next line: "But it was not necessary for me to open that letter because I knew what was in it."

The letter that Dad was fearful of opening contained a draft questionnaire. My father knew he was going to be drafted into the military, and this letter was part of the early induction process. While I was aware of Dad's service to his country, what this speech revealed next came very much as a surprise.

Dad made clear in his address he thought a war between the United States and Russia would be "wrong." Just three and half years after the end of World War II, he felt the world had already "seen too much carnage and slaughter." Because of this, he believed he "had to be a conscientious objector."

I was taken aback. I had no idea Dad had ever considered refusing to serve. Suddenly, the speech's title made sense: "A State of Mind." Dad was pulling back the curtains on what was going on in his twenty-one-year-old head. He had serious reservations about being drafted and taking part in any conflict. But just when I thought I knew where the speech was headed, Dad took a detour.

After months of agonizing, my father realized he was not—in his words—"courageous enough" to be a conscientious objector. Later in his speech, he revealed he had indeed registered for the draft. But while Dad gave in to conscription, his objections to armed conflict did not simply go away. And this is where the detour came in.

Halfway through his remarks, Dad made a shrewd and subtle shift. As the *Daily Northwestern* described it, "Vanocur's address was [also] a severe criticism of the 'American democratic philosophy of force.'" In other words, Dad was waging verbal war against war itself. He was no longer just describing his own state of mind; he was also talking about the country's state of mind as well. As he put it, "Today the state of mind this nation has accepted [is] the inevitability of war."

But despite the personal anguish he felt over war and his imminent service in the Army, Dad's speech was not devoid of hope. He told the contest judges and a crowd of several hundred that war was neither desirable or inevitable. He much preferred a world where freedom triumphed force.

Dad ended his speech with these dramatic words:

"It is human dignity or human misery.

"It is freedom or it is force.

"It is all a state of mind."[4]

I found myself fascinated not just by what Dad said in this speech, but also by what it said about him. Again, for a young man to express himself in such a passionate yet cogent manner was impressive to me. His promise as a keen political observer was already in full bloom.

By comparison, when I was twenty-one and also a student at Northwestern, nobody—and I mean nobody—was giving me any awards for my speaking abilities. Or, to be more precise, my inability to speak. My state of mind at the time was much more focused on sorority coeds than international conflicts.

---

4. Vanocur, "A State of Mind," speech.

Dad's speech also showed his competitive nature. Not only did he compete against the best speakers at Northwestern (which had its own School of Speech) but also against the top orators in the Midwest. Dad and I never really discussed his or my competitiveness. But, as I would later discover in his study, we both viewed other reporters, even those we worked with, as despised rivals.

For each of these oratorical contests, Dad won a hundred-dollar prize. This $200 total would be worth roughly ten times that amount today. Not a bad payday for a college kid. This money foreshadowed a fairly lucrative future side hustle for my father. Looking at all the speaking contracts I found in his study, I was amazed at how many speeches he gave all over the country. The money he received for these numerous speeches was not insignificant.

The "State of Mind" speech also highlighted what would be a recurring subject in Dad's life and career: the threat of communism. In the next decade and a half, he would both fight communism and report on it. This is why this line toward the end of his speech was particularly noteworthy: "The battle for freedom will not be fought in the Kremlin, nor will it be fought in the Pentagon. It will be fought with food and ideas in the rice paddies of China and the fields of Indonesia." I was especially struck by this mention of rice paddies in Southeast Asia. Dad didn't know it at the time, but it wouldn't be long before he found himself reporting from Vietnam.

It wasn't lost on me that I had ended up learning a lot from a speech I initially threw away. Fortunately, I screwed up early in the process. Moving forward, I knew I would have to painstakingly review every single piece of paper in his study. As I attempted to finally figure out who my father really was and why he was such a dominant force in shaping my life, I would need as many clues as I could find.

Dad's eloquent words from 1949 gave me a good start. They provided an insightful and valuable glimpse into his life as a young man. But they also yielded another unexpected gift.

As I read my father's speech, I could hear his voice delivering it. Having listened to a number of his speeches in person, it was easy for me to imagine his delivery and cadence. To do so now was especially comforting. Dad's dementia and condition had been worsening of late, making it harder and harder for him to express himself. His speaking had been mostly reduced to short phrases or confused questions. Discovering this nearly seventy-year-old speech allowed me to hear Dad in all his eloquence. Being transported back to this happier place and time did much to ease my own state of mind.

Chapter Two

B+ Student

My parents thought I was retarded.

Yes, I know, that's now a politically incorrect word to use.

But back in the early sixties, it was much more commonly accepted. Those were the years when my parents were genuinely worried about me. They were concerned I might be impaired or challenged. My childhood development just seemed slower in comparison to the other kids. It took me longer to grasp concepts and figure things out. This might help explain why I "flunked" kindergarten and had to do it twice.

Oddly, though, my parents never bothered to tell me about any of this. I would only learn of their concerns decades later by accident.

I was well into adulthood when the truth slipped out. It happened at a family dinner. Dad was telling some unrelated story and unwittingly used the phrase, "You know, it was about the time we thought there was something wrong with Chris."

I was busy eating, and I nearly choked on my food when he said my name. Yet I somehow managed to swallow both my mouthful and my pride and asked for more details.

Dad initially responded somewhat matter-of-factly, implying it hadn't really been that big of a deal. But he eventually confessed my sluggish childhood development had sparked some serious discussions between him and my mother. So much so that one night, they had an animated debate about it. This frustrated my father and motivated him to settle the matter once and for all.

He explained to me how he held up a single finger in front of my face and told me to follow it with my eyes. As he moved the finger from side to side, I dutifully eyeballed his wagging digit. With that, Dad proudly turned to my mother and said, "See. I told you he was fine."

Let's recap, shall we?

My parents thought there was something wrong with me.

They never told me about their concerns.

This was the highly scientific cognitive exam they used to test me.

Fortunately, I can laugh at all this now. Kind of. But there are actually some key points to be made here. First, I sort of understand why my folks were worried about me. The truth is, I have always been a bit different. I just don't see the world in traditional ways.

For example...

When I was being tested for a prestigious Washington, D.C., preschool, the examiners gave me some wooden building blocks to play with. They then asked if I knew what a bridge was. When I said yes, they wanted to know if I could use those wooden blocks to build a bridge. I shook my head and said no. My negative answer took them aback. When the surprised school administrators asked me why not, I simply told them, "It isn't a bridge building day." Miraculously, I was accepted for admission.

But here's the crucial point to be made here. While I can be a bit slow on the uptake, I eventually figure things out. What's more, after I figure them out, I often excel. Proof of this, unexpectedly, turned up in my father's study.

In a folder conspicuously marked "Chris Vanocur," I found an official correspondence from Northwestern University. It notified my father that I had made the honor roll with a 4.0 grade point average. It was curiously the only thing in the folder. But I was genuinely touched he had proudly held on to it for more than thirty years.

However, to be absolutely clear, I was neither a very good student in high school and college nor a very bad one. My GPA often fluctuated. 4.0

was the ceiling and 2.67 was the floor. My poor college entrance exam scores were nothing to brag about either. I ended up with a cumulative GPA of about 3.4. In other words, I was a B+ student. Respectable but by no means outstanding.

In high school, math was my nemesis. I was actually pretty good with numbers until Algebra torpedoed me. I also had the same dismal result with Geometry. I got C's in these subjects and needed special tutors just to achieve those subpar marks. Coincidentally, the first time in high school I didn't have to take a math class, I also made the honor roll. Why we force some students to take advanced math classes when basic financial literacy would be so much more useful is one of my pet peeves.

In college, it was déjà vu all over again. Pretty good grades with one blemish. But this time it wasn't math that sunk me; it was a girl. In the springtime of my freshman year, I fell hard for the girl who took my virginity (I was a late bloomer at age nineteen). Unfortunately, it turned out she just wasn't that into me. This led to some heartbreak on my end and a mild downward spiral. I spent too many nights drowning my sorrows. This caused me to oversleep and miss some early classes. My GPA fell below 3.0. While this romantic ennui wasn't ultimately catastrophic, it's also not a time in my life I am particularly proud of.

Fortunately, I spent that summer working at Glacier National Park in Montana. Its otherworldly natural beauty helped rejuvenate me and put me back on the straight and narrow. It would also be the reason I decided to live much of my life in the West.

A couple of enduring academic strengths would help bail me out over the years. First, I always did well in history and English classes. For reasons still unclear to me, my writing has always been pretty good.

Of even more importance, though, was something I had in common with my father: we both worked exceedingly hard. While I didn't come close to achieving his academic distinction, it wasn't necessarily because of a lack of effort. Except for the above-mentioned female distraction, I always put in the hours at school. I was just wired to be a bookworm.

My last quarter in college is a good case in point. When spring finally arrived after another bitterly cold winter in Chicago, a number of my classmates came down with a bad case of senioritis. Lacking motivation, attendance was, perhaps, somewhat down in classes and up in outdoor keggers.

But not me. For whatever reason, I bore down even harder. That's when I got the 4.0 GPA that made Dad so proud. This included an A in an English class about Dickens and an A in Rhetorical History of the '60s. The latter was one of my favorite college classes. Interestingly, before one lecture, the professor quietly let me know he would be mentioning my father—specifically, a memorable question Dad had asked in the first Kennedy-Nixon debate.

But it was in another of my spring classes where my college drive and late-blooming were really on display. It was a special seminar on the Spanish Civil War. For most of the class, I was hopelessly lost. I just couldn't keep straight exactly who was fighting who and, for that matter, why. A firmer understanding of this information really would have been quite useful. But fortunately, our entire grade was based on a paper written at the end of the term. While most of the class wrote traditional academic essays, I took a different approach.

I had long been fascinated by one of Pablo Picasso's masterpieces, *Guernica*. Its vivid and stark depictions of modern warfare had left a lasting impression on me. Not only did the painting shine a worldwide spotlight on the Spanish Civil War, it had also come to be regarded as a classic anti-war work of art. Accordingly, I found myself extremely curious about why this painting became so well known. I wanted to know exactly why its hold on people was so indelible. So, that's what I wrote about. I stayed true to Dad's advice that the small stories in life are the best.

Night after night in the old section of the Northwestern Library, I burrowed myself in a big stack of art and history books. I didn't care that I was going to graduate regardless of what grade I got on the paper. I found myself obsessed with the subject. This tunnel vision would become a trait that would serve me well as a reporter, but perhaps poorly as a person.

One particular episode during this time shows just how focused I was on the paper. On a warm spring evening, I again headed to the library to do additional research. En route, I happened to run into a lovely classmate with whom I had a nodding acquaintance. As we neared the library, she coyly suggested skipping the library, getting some ice cream, and going for a romantic sunset walk by the lake. In a moment of complete idiocy, I told her I couldn't because I had work to do. She looked at me with mild disappointment and disbelief. I have regretted my youthful non-indiscretion to this day. But this awkward moment illustrated a key recurring theme in my life: I almost always put work first.

For better or worse, my industriousness and celibacy were soon rewarded. When the grades were handed out for the Spanish Civil War papers, I got an A+. This was the only time in my academic career I received such a lofty mark.

The *Guernica* paper also highlighted another of my traits. Specifically, my tendency to look where others didn't. While other classmates were writing about the political and military minutia of the war, I wrote about a painting. It wasn't an obvious choice, but it was a highly successful one. While my parents were once concerned because I viewed the world differently, I came to see it as a sort of superpower. One which, decades later, helped me break the biggest story of my reporting career.

Before we mercifully end this discussion of my not-always-stellar academic career, I must thank my father for his generosity. Whether it was paying for my tuition at the Sidwell Friends School in Washington, D.C., at Northwestern, or even for my junior year studying abroad at the University of Edinburgh in Scotland, Dad always generously footed the bill. I was both lucky and privileged in this regard and am eternally grateful for his kind and magnanimous support. But my gratitude also comes with some guilt. Even after all these years, I find myself chagrined I was only a B+ student. I remain somewhat embarrassed by the notion I could and should have done better.

Amusingly, though, in my later life, I would occasionally run into some of the people Dad worked with at ABC News. When they found out I was Sander Vanocur's son, they would start to laugh. They would then good-naturedly explain why, saying something like, "Oh, you must be the one with the college tuition bills your dad was always complaining about." Instead of being mad or hurt, I shared in their mirth and in their genuine affection for my father.

By the way, for those who might be wondering, I most definitely did not enter any oratorical contests while in college. I did, however, happen to take one speechwriting class.

I got an A.

CHAPTER THREE

Forever Lost to the Law

WHEN SEBASTIAN HAFFNER wrote his February 11 article for the (London) *Sunday Observer* in 1951, he unwittingly unleashed a powerful dynamic unto the world. Specifically, he helped launch the career of one of America's most respected television reporters.

The headline for Haffner's column was, "WORLD POWER TO-MORROW." It was a cautionary piece, one warning English readers of the possible dangers of America's rearmament after World War II. Haffner wrote that America's growing military strength would "mean the greatest shift in world power seen this century." He ended by taking this prediction one step further, suggesting that a powerful America would be without equal in the world.[5]

This column did not sit well with a twenty-three-year-old Sander Vanocur. After graduating from Northwestern, Dad studied international politics at the London School of Economics. He mentioned to his tutor he was angry about what Haffner had written. So, the tutor suggested Dad write a response to Haffner's article. Little did this long-ago English instructor realize, but his suggestion would change my father's life and strongly influence mine.

Within just a few days, Dad had crafted a highly effective response to Haffner's column. He then gave it to the *Observer*, and the prestigious newspaper published it the very next Sunday. Dad's piece was called "TWO WORLD POWERS." Underneath, his byline read:

---

5. Haffner, "World Power."

By SANDER VANOCUR
Graduate of North-Western [sic] University, Illinois

My father began his article by wondering if an American might be allowed to question "Mr. Haffner's reasoning, and to ask whether his picture is not over-simplified."

Dad went on to argue that America was not the world's only superpower. As proof, he cited the imminent threat posed by the Soviet Union. He then outlined in well-reasoned detail why Russia was so dangerous. My father even cited Alexis de Tocqueville, the French philosopher who believed the two countries had long marched in lockstep, one seeking democracy, the other power. Dad eloquently ended his piece by arguing that we very much lived in a two-power world.[6]

If I may offer a not-so-humble brag about Pop, it was an exceptionally artful and well-constructed column. The fact he was only twenty-three when he wrote it astounded me. And I'm not the only one who gave it rave reviews.

In one of Dad's oldest files, I discovered a letter dated February 17, 1951. This would have been after my father had finished writing his article but before it had been published. The letter was from one of the higher-ups at the *Observer*. In a typically British sort of understated way, it compliments my dad on his work: "I think the article makes an excellent feature and I'm very glad you came along to write it."

Some editors even took my father to a celebratory lunch at the historic Savoy Hotel. For his efforts, my father was paid seventeen pounds for writing the *Observer* article. Ultimately, though, it would be worth much more than that.

My father's February 18 article effectively kickstarted what would be a long and distinguished journalism career. Dad had planned on returning

6. Vanocur, "Two World Powers."

to America and becoming a lawyer. He said several times in various interviews that he even had a law school scholarship waiting for him back at Northwestern. His father was an attorney, and it couldn't have been hard to imagine Sander Vanocur ending up as a senior partner at a big Chicago law firm. After all, my father was once perfectly described as being "canny," someone who would have been a success in whatever profession he chose.

But Dad's response to Sebastian Haffner changed everything. My father often said when he first saw his name in print, he was "forever lost to the law." It's a charming and effective line. It simultaneously discarded the perceived mustiness of being a lawyer while plunging headfirst into the adrenaline-inducing world of journalism. However, I later wondered whether Dad, in seeing his name in print, was also seduced by the first whispers of fame.

I've also occasionally contemplated what would have happened to me if Dad had become a lawyer. With him being such a powerful role model, would I have become an attorney too? The answer likely would have been no.

To paraphrase John Houseman in *The Paper Chase*, I had serious doubts about me ever becoming a lawyer.[7] I took one pre-law class at Northwestern and struggled. Not unlike the problems I had remembering exactly who fought in the Spanish Civil War, I had trouble recalling and citing Supreme Court cases. I managed to squeak out an acceptable grade in the class (maybe a B+), but I didn't really enjoy it all that much. After my academic difficulties there, the law was lost to me as well.

Even though I reread Dad's *Observer* piece many times, one thing still puzzled me. I didn't know why Haffner's words angered my father so much. It didn't necessarily seem the type of Op-Ed that would elicit such a strong rebuttal.

So, during a break from sifting through Dad's study, I walked back down to the house and showed him his *Observer* article. I hoped he would be

7. *The Paper Chase*, 1973.

able to shed some light on why he wrote it. Instead, he simply stared at it for a long time. Finally, he handed it back to me, smiled, and said, "I wish I still wrote that well."

Left to my own devices, I tried to deconstruct Dad's motivation for rebutting Haffner. Maybe it was his training as a topflight debater. Dad, after all, was well practiced when it came to making a counter-argument. He was also a smart enough student of politics and history to be able to back up his argument. While these explanations seemed plausible, they weren't necessarily satisfying. I couldn't help but think something else was at play here.

Ultimately, this is what I came up with. My father always had a heightened sense of what he felt was right and wrong in the world. I'm not quite sure where this journalistic and personal righteousness came from, but it surfaced again and again in his reporting career. Viewers and politicians could see it in his dispatches from Vietnam, as well as in his coverage of the civil rights movement.

Perhaps Dad thought Haffner's piece wasn't just inaccurate or misguided, but also potentially dangerous. Maybe he thought it was imperative to warn the world about the Soviet Union and communism. (It should also be noted here that it's quite possible I inherited this moralistic streak as well.)

Although my father was smitten with journalism after his successful *Observer* column, his reporting aspirations had to be put on hold. He was finally inducted into military service and eventually assigned to an Army intelligence unit in Berlin.

It was only after Lt. Vanocur's military obligations were finished that he could return to England to begin his journalism career in earnest. Characteristically, he threw himself into his work. He not only landed a job with the *Manchester Guardian*, but also found time to do commentary for the BBC, some work as a stringer for CBS, and weekend writing for the United Press International (UPI).

For all these jobs, Dad earned about $125 a month. In a later interview, he said this monthly stipend allowed him to live like "a king." His rose-colored memories of his youthful English days reminded me of my own time studying in Scotland. After finishing my enchanting junior year studying abroad at the University of Edinburgh, I wasn't sure I wanted to go back to the States either.

And the similarities between the two of us continued after we both returned to America. Dad would be fired from his first stateside reporting job. I would be let go from my first TV post as well. Little did either of us know that both of these firings would turn out to be blessings in disguise.

Chapter Four

Fired from the *New York Times*

The *New York Times* fired my father in 1957.

Dad had mentioned this dismissal several times over the years but never really explained why the newspaper let him go. Rummaging around his study, however, led me to the truth.

Dad joined the *Times* in 1955. Given his recent time in Europe, he hoped to be assigned as an overseas reporter. Instead, as he put it, they sent him over the East River to be a crime reporter in Queens.

In an old folder marked simply, "NY Times SV," the pieces of the puzzle began to come together. Inside was a letter that helped explain Dad's departure from the paper, as well as some of his articles.

The letter is dated September 13, 1957, and is signed by a Richard D. Burritt, Administrative Assistant to the Managing Editor. I immediately recognized the old-school font on the top of the letter, "The New York Times" and the address just below, "Times Square."

This letter was just over a page long. It was addressed to:

Mr. Sander Vanocur
105-10 62nd Road
Forest Hills, Queens, L.I., N.Y.

Dear Mr. Vanocur,
This is a letter I would like to give you before you leave us...

As you know, we now have, and for some years have had, a recruiting practice that is two-fold in character. We hire likely young men as copy boys, move the best ones into clerical positions as the opportunity arises, and, again as the opportunity arises, give our best clerks a crack at reporting. When we hire from the outside, we take men who already have records of substantial accomplishment on some of our better newspapers, or they come from wire services. I am sure you will recognize several men from both categories on the staff now.

Your case was different. You were younger than most reporters coming to us from the outside. You had less newspaper experience, yet you were a mature man and had had experience on at least one newspaper and in radio and television in England.

It was frankly a case of your being neither "fish nor fowl" when you came to the staff. You were neither a beginner in the sense of the young men that we have been promoting from within, nor a seasoned man in the sense of the men we have been taking from the outside.

It is my sincere belief that you were caught to your disadvantage in the mechanics of a situation that was bigger than yourself or any one individual involved. I genuinely regret this, feel a sense of failure on my part as a personnel man, and am sorry about your departure from the staff.

I assure you in this letter, as I have already done orally, that you are respected and liked in the newsroom of The New York Times.[8]

Later in the study, I found a lengthy transcript of an interview Dad had done later in his career. He described a conversation he'd had with an editor at the *Times,* one who had been assigned to help him with his writing. The editor told my father, "Vanocur, you have a big problem here at the *New York Times.*" My father asked him what the problem was. The

8. Burritt to Vanocur, 1957.

editor said, "Your writing is too colloquial. You write like people talk and that's unacceptable at the *New York Times*."

Knowing this, I went back to Dad's old *NY Times* folder and read some of his stories. And, yes, his writing sometimes might be considered colloquial. But that wasn't my main takeaway from the articles he had saved.

Most were short pieces about various petty crimes in Queens. Only two of these articles had his byline. One was about the destruction of some old sycamore trees. The other had this curious headline: "1,000 CELEBRATE WIENER-BEER DAY."

It turns out one of Dad's big byline stories was about how German-American Day was celebrated in North Bergen, New Jersey. The story was accompanied by a picture of a prominent New Jersey politician apparently about to launch a frankfurter into his mouth. The lede to his article matched the photograph. Dad's opening line described those of German descent "dedicating themselves" to the consumption of many meat-filled tubes, washed down with copious amounts of beer.[9]

Just a few years after Dad left Army intelligence in Berlin, he was covering German-American day and bratwurst. And that, I quickly concluded, was the real problem for my father at the *New York Times*.

Dad wasn't just smart; he was quite ambitious as well. Reading the articles in the folder made me think the *Times* hadn't necessarily made the best use of his intellect or talents. Having covered many of these types of stories myself, Dad's assignments struck me as being a bit provincial. This was, after all, a young man who had just come from Fleet Street in London, studying at the London School of Economics, and writing about the complexities of American-Russian relations. Now, he was being assigned to stories about hot dogs and beer. Yes, it was for the *New York Times*, but I kept thinking my father would have been capable of so much more.

To bolster my theory about Dad being underutilized, I went online

9. Vanocur, "Wiener-Beer Day."

looking for more of his stories at the *Times*. But I was unable to find any. Luckily, though, I discovered something equally intriguing. It was an excerpt from Gay Talese's *The Kingdom and the Power: Behind the Scenes at The New York Times: The Institution That Influences the World.*

Talese wrote that a young reporter at the *Times* was expected to stay at his "desk near the back of the newsroom and await his turn." He also wrote that, for a young reporter like my father, showing too much initiative could actually be a bad thing.[10] Talese's writing confirmed my suspicions that my father was frustrated with his role at the *Times*. Patience has never exactly been Dad's strongest suit. Or mine.

My father later admitted to being crushed when the *Times* told him he was being let go. To be as intelligent as he was, and with his drive and ambition, this must have seemed like a huge setback. Having been given this kind of opportunity with this kind of newspaper, I suspect Dad thought he had failed. This must have been intolerable for him, especially given all the success and achievements he had known as a young man in school and in Europe.

But this setback was about more than just wounded pride. Dad was now nearly thirty years old, married, and with a newborn child (my brother). I can only imagine what kind of pressure he was under to find work.

Fortunately, as my father would later tell me, he knew somebody at the National Broadcasting Company. It must have been a good contact because Dad soon went to work for NBC News. And, as Talese noted, it wouldn't be long before my father was acknowledged as being one of the best reporters in America.

---

10. Talese, *The Kingdom and the Power.*

Chapter Five

Like Father, Like Son

THIRTY-THREE YEARS AFTER my father was fired by the *New York Times*, I was fired from my first journalism job.

I was working as an on-air TV reporter for one of the local stations in Salt Lake City. Utah wasn't necessarily my first choice of where to live, but the economy wasn't in great shape when I graduated college in the summer of 1982. So, I accepted the job (which Dad helped arrange). I thought I would stay there for a couple of years and then move to a bigger TV market. My first assignment was as an associate producer for one of the early morning newscasts. Then, over the course of a few months, I made my way up the ladder. Eventually, I became a full-time reporter.

But despite this steady rise through the ranks, the truth is I wasn't very good in my early years. I found the transition from college student to a young, low-paid TV journalist challenging. Academia had been my cocoon for most of my life, and I had to learn how to adapt outside of it. Fortunately, Dad had advised me to treat the first two years in Salt Lake as a kind of journalism graduate school. I would learn the trade and actually get paid for it.

This is not to say that there weren't some bumps along the way. I made all the typical blunders "green" reporters make. I asked stupid questions, I flubbed live shots right and left, and I somehow managed to screw up a story about Santa on Christmas. I also may have been the world's worst crime reporter ever. I missed story after story on that beat until the station mercifully took me off it.

I was so bad that my news director said I was on the longest evolutionary track of any reporter he had ever worked with. Sound familiar? I was slow to adapt to a new situation. It was just like kindergarten, high school, and college. It took me a while to "get" things.

One of my biggest problems was my delivery, the narration on my stories. I spoke too slowly or in too much of a monotone. One consultant described my delivery as "choppy." I just couldn't get the proper cadence down. Instead of being relaxed, my narration sounded uptight and forced. Dad was fired for sounding too conversational, and I was hindered by not sounding conversational enough. Although my delivery would improve over the course of my career, it never reached a point where I was happy with it. I think it's one of the main reasons my career stalled out at the local level and I never made it to any of the networks.

Despite these initial struggles, I kept plugging away. I ended up lasting eight years at my first station before I got fired. But the real irony was they let me go just as I was starting to get pretty good. Not long before I got fired, I received several job offers from other stations. I also won my first Emmy award. But then office politics got in the way.

The station wanted me to move back to my hometown and take over its Washington, D.C., bureau. However, I had already done a brief stint in the bureau working with Lucky Severson, who would later move on to one of the national networks. While I learned several valuable lessons from Lucky—like never give your best lines to an anchor—I didn't really love reporting in D.C. There were already so many journalists there, and I worried whether I would be able to carve out my own niche. So, I ultimately told the station I didn't want to go.

I don't know if this refusal to go to D.C. was the reason I got fired, but I don't think it helped. I was, like Dad, sometimes stubborn, headstrong, and a bit opinionated. When the newsroom had to lay off several staffers because of budget cuts, I was terminated.

Being fired was devastating. The station was in a remote industrial area, and I went for a long walk after getting canned. Tears streamed down my face as I walked on an unfinished road. I was in my early thirties, roughly the same age as my father when he was fired. I was convinced I was a failure. I felt like I was nothing more than an unemployed, mediocre local reporter in a medium-sized TV market. I dreaded telling my father the news.

But fortunately, like Dad, I quickly found another job. Just hours after I had been fired, I got a call from John Edwards. He was the news director at one of the other Salt Lake TV stations and the man who really salvaged my career. Several people on his staff had strongly urged him to hire me and let him know what a hard worker I was. So, about ten days later, I signed on. Albeit with a significant pay cut.

Once again, my life and career were mirroring my father's trajectory. When he left the *New York Times* to go NBC, he went from being a self-perceived failure to being a star. Similarly, my firing and a change of scenery allowed me to flourish. My new boss, as it turned out, wanted me to be the station's political reporter. And just like my dad, it was when I started covering politics that I finally found my true calling.

Chapter Six

JFK—Part One

One of the more intriguing items I found in Dad's study was an NBC souvenir booklet from the sixties. I'm guessing it was given to network sponsors, affiliates, and TV critics around the country. In addition to promising that two-thirds of its programming would be in color, inside were pictures and blurbs about some of NBC's biggest stars: Bob Hope, Johnny Carson, Walt Disney, and Mr. Magoo. Comedian Johnathan Winters was also included. This made me smile. Not only do I have fond memories of watching Winters with my dad, but the comedian also lived in Montecito. Sometimes he and my father would cross friendly paths. Occasionally, the two were even mistaken for each other.

I also smiled when I got to the section promoting NBC's well-regarded news division. There, on page ninety-three, was a nice black and white portrait of my dad. And accompanying his picture was a short yet fascinating bio:

> *Early in 1960, NBC News assigned Sander Vanocur, then its man in Chicago, to cover the primary campaign of Senator John Kennedy. Rarely has there been more inspired matchmaking of newsman and newsmaker. For Kennedy and Vanocur hit it off at once and formed a deep friendship. Vanocur covered every Kennedy primary, the conventions and the campaign. Upon Kennedy's victory, Vanocur became an NBC White House correspondent.*[11]

11. NBC souvenir booklet, 93.

The tone of this bio surprised me. Specifically, that NBC played up how close my father and President Kennedy were. The terms "inspired matchmaking" and "deep friendship" caught me off guard. I understood why NBC wanted to promote my dad and his relationship with Kennedy; Kennedy was good for ratings. But calling attention to their friendly relationship still struck me as odd. Here was one of America's prominent news networks actively promoting how close my father was to a Democratic president. I couldn't help but think in today's era of partisan trench warfare, Republicans would have had a field day with NBC's choice of words.

The Kennedy-Vanocur arranged marriage was very much the result of one man's actions. His name was Reuven Frank, the producer of *The Huntley-Brinkley Report* and later the president of NBC News. He was a mentor of sorts to my dad over the years, especially at the beginning of his career. Although the two would squabble now and then, they would stay in touch long after both men had left NBC.

On one of Dad's many bookcases in his study, I happened upon a copy of Frank's book, *Out of Thin Air: The Brief Wonderful Life of Network News*. In it, Frank described his attempts to get NBC's newest hire to become the network's Midwest correspondent: "He [Vanocur] was midwestern born and bred, and nothing ever happened in Chicago anymore."[12] Eventually, my dad signed on after being convinced he would be able to cover everything, regardless of where it was happening.

And everything included the 1960 presidential campaign.

In one of Dad's many files on the Kennedys, I found the transcripts of several lengthy interviews he did for the JFK Library as part of the JFK Oral History Collection. In them, Dad talks about meeting John F. Kennedy for the first time in a Las Vegas hotel in 1960: "I think it was [at] the Sands or the Dunes—I can't remember which."

Dad described running into Kennedy with this wonderful anecdote:

12. Frank, *Out of Thin Air*.

"It was the first time I met Kennedy... He was wandering around the crap tables. We came face to face, and I introduced myself, and I thought—I could be wrong—that he wanted to shoot dice. He looked longingly at the tables, I thought."

Given how many people associate my father with the Kennedys, I was surprised to learn Dad wasn't necessarily all that impressed with JFK at first. In another interview transcript I found, Dad was asked what his first impression was of the Massachusetts senator. He said JFK was "[a] terrible speaker, terribly nervous, but he seemed to resonate with people because he seemed to hold out some kind of promise to what they thought was the promised land."[13]

Minnesota Senator Hubert Humphrey was also running for president in 1960, and Dad covered him as well. Humphrey was a politician my father had known for several years and greatly admired. In fact, when Humphrey was vice president, my father made sure my brother and I got our pictures taken with him. I still have that photo more than a half century later.

In Dad's study, I also found several copies of *The Reporter Magazine*. In the March 17, 1960, issue, my father wrote an article called "Humphrey vs. Kennedy: High Stakes in Wisconsin." In it, he explained why Wisconsin had become the most important Democratic primary that year and a place where the two candidates' ambitions "[would] be tested."

While my father enthusiastically praised Humphrey in the article, he also gave Kennedy his due. Dad mentioned the bigger crowds JFK was drawing, as well as the star quality of Jackie Kennedy on the campaign trail. He also paid Kennedy what I thought was a rather interesting sort of compliment. After describing Kennedy as being charismatic and good-looking, Dad also noted JFK was "perhaps as ruthless as any Boston ward leader."[14]

To me, this is vintage Vanocur. Dad was direct, accurate, and prescient. While many were already becoming caught up in the Kennedy mystique,

13. Vanocur, interview, Freedom Forum.
14. Vanocur, "Humphrey vs. Kennedy."

my father wasn't. He wasn't afraid to describe Kennedy as he saw him, the good and the not so good. In fact, Dad would later say this *Reporter* article had angered Kennedy. Dad thought Kennedy didn't like him writing about how much money his campaign was spending in Wisconsin.

The more I read about Dad's relationship with JFK, and later with Robert Kennedy, a trend began to emerge. There were moments of genuine affection, but also some heated exchanges, often when Dad confronted them professionally.

"Get to Chicago."

This was the urgent instruction NBC News gave to my father in September of 1960. Dad was in Jackson, Mississippi, covering the presidential campaign of Richard Nixon. Dad got the marching orders to head back home because he had been picked to be NBC's panelist in the Kennedy-Nixon debate on September 26th. It would be the first televised presidential debate in U.S. history. As part of the JFK Oral History interview, Dad said, "I went to the hotel, had a steam bath, made myself a reservation on the Panama Limited, had a swell dinner, and I went to my room and started writing questions."

I loved the fact Dad mentioned the steam bath, the name of the train, and even that he remembered there was a yellow rose on his table in the dining car. Over the years, his memory of small details like this helped make him a compelling storyteller.

Arriving in Chicago the next day, Dad said, "[I] was met by my wife and two kids. My littlest boy"— me!—"who had been born on November 5th, I had hardly seen except for a short period in the spring, because I had gone out to cover Nelson Rockefeller four days after she went to the hospital, and it was great being home."

Reading this gave me some pause. I had been born in November of 1959, and here it was September 1960. In the course of nearly a year, my only extended time with my father appears to have been for a short stretch in the spring. Having been in the same business, I all too well understood the time restraints news reporters were under. Still, I was a bit taken aback to learn how little Dad had actually been around during my first year.

As for the debate itself, it literally changed the fortunes of John F. Kennedy, Richard M. Nixon, and my father. This was the moment my favorite college professor had deemed so vital that he included it in one of his lectures.

About fifteen minutes into the debate, after the opening statements, the debate panelists introduced themselves. One by one, the four questioners turned in their chairs, looked at the cameras, and introduced themselves. Dad went first, saying simply, "I'm Sander Vanocur, NBC News." Years later, he would write in a *Boston.com* article that he did not "realize that I was part of a great historic event that day."[15]

But just ten minutes later, Dad's role would forever be etched into political history. He addressed a question to Vice President Nixon. Watching it on YouTube now, I can tell my father was a bit nervous. Being such an accomplished public speaker, he would rarely say "uh" even once when talking. But in his question to Nixon, Dad said it several times. Nevertheless, it was the substance of the question that viewers and the vice president would remember.

Here is the question taken directly from a transcript of that 1960 debate:

> MR. VANOCUR: Uh—Mr. Vice President, since the question of executive leadership is a very important campaign issue, I'd like to follow Mr. Novins' question. Now, Republican campaign slogans—you'll see them on signs around the country as you did last week—say it's experience that counts—that's over a picture of yourself; sir uh—implying that you've had more governmental executive decision-making uh—experience than uh—your

15. Vanocur, "Debates have come a long way since 1960."

opponent. Now, in his news conference on August twenty-fourth, President Eisenhower was asked to give one example of a major idea of yours that he adopted. His reply was, and I'm quoting; 'If you give me a week I might think of one. I don't remember.' Now that was a month ago, sir, and the President hasn't brought it up since, and I'm wondering, sir, if you can clarify which version is correct—the one put out by Republican campaign leaders or the one put out by President Eisenhower?

MR. NIXON: Well, I would suggest, Mr. Vanocur, that uh—if you know the President, that was probably a facetious remark.[16]

Nixon's response was accompanied by what might be described as a forced smile. He would go on to try and answer the question, but the political damage had already been done. One colleague would later tell Dad it was the "toughest question he had ever heard a reporter ask a politician."

In his JFK Oral History interview, Dad said he was told "that in the press room at WBBM in Chicago, when I asked the question the press corps broke into cheers or applause. But I worked goddamn hard on that question, and it was the most glaring question one could ask. I thought I asked Kennedy a good question, though in comparison it didn't even match. But Nixon would never forgive me for that question."

Dad's question was so damaging, it would eventually live rent-free in Nixon's head. In his book *Six Crises*, Nixon wrote that it was a question "of no real substantive importance actually—[which] was to plague me the rest of the campaign."

Later, in the same book, Nixon conceded the question was effective in raising doubts about his experience.[17]

My dad was only thirty-two years old when he asked Vice President

16. Kennedy vs. Nixon, 1960 Presidential Debate.
17. Nixon, *Six Crises*.

Nixon that unforgettable debate question. He also had only a few years of TV experience. But this question, as well as his campaign and convention coverage, quickly established him as one of the rising news stars on the new medium of television. For his hard work and his obvious potential, my father would soon be named a White House correspondent for NBC.

But before that part of the story, two quick final notes about the debate.

Dad's question would become so legendary that Nixon's attempted answer about it being a "facetious remark" actually ended up being used in a *Simpsons* episode. I think that made my father proud, even though I'm not entirely convinced he knew who the Simpsons were.

The final anecdote about my father and the debate deals with the notes Kennedy took that night. Somehow, Dad ended up with JFK's debate notes. Several months later, the new president was kind enough to inscribe those notes for my father. President Kennedy wrote, "For Sandy—with esteem and warm regards from his friend John F. Kennedy."[18]

This gracious note seemed to confirm the "deep friendship" the NBC News promotional booklet touted. But, in some ways, this was just the beginning of their relationship. Dad still had miles to go in his journey with JFK and the rest of the Kennedys.

---

18. Kennedy to Vanocur, February 1961.

Chapter Seven

JFK—Part Two

Among the many curious items in Dad's study was the fifty-five-year-old deed to our first house in Washington, D.C. It struck me as a bit peculiar that he still had it. We hadn't lived there for a half a century.

This somewhat smallish house was located on Ordway Street in a comely part of Northwest Washington. My family had moved to the nation's capital when I was a little over a year old. Dad would have just been turning thirty-three. It bears repeating that only four years earlier, he had been fired from his first stateside reporting job, and his future in journalism was much in doubt. But now, he worked for a prominent news network and was headed to the White House to cover the country's first "TV president."

As he would later tell the JFK Library's Oral History program, "I came to Washington; I bought a house, a red Studebaker, which turned out to be a lemon... and a #29 red shag rug for my kids' bedroom from Sears and Roebuck, and my wife and I were broke. Not a nickel."

I loved the fact Dad would remember and use a phrase like a "#29 red shag rug from Sears." The little details he wove into stories never ceased to amaze me. He often used similar nugget-sized anecdotes to help create lasting images for many TV viewers.

This was also another example of Dad telling whoever would listen that he was broke. In this case, he shared his financial woes with the Kennedy Library. While some of it may have been hyperbole, there was also some truth to it. My father often stretched himself too thin financially.

Every now and then, my father would tell me about growing up during the Great Depression. He explained how this had strongly influenced his relationship with money. He simply wasn't used to having a lot of it around. So, when he got some cash, he spent it. Being broke was kind of his default setting. Although he earned a fair amount in his career, he consistently had trouble holding on to it.

This was one of the rare ways my father and I couldn't have been more different. I tended to save every penny that came my way. My parents used to tease me by saying I was the only person they knew who would be perfectly happy walking around for a few weeks with only a handful of dollars in their pocket. To that frugal point, one year they gave me one hundred dollars for my birthday. Accompanying this generous present was a wry note that simply said, "Please do something irresponsible with this money." In my defense, I wouldn't characterize myself as cheap. I instead prefer to call myself "value-driven."

Dad and I also reacted quite differently to new assignments and opportunities. While I was plodding and slow to react to new challenges, my father was a quick study. When it came to covering the White House, he plunged eagerly into his new assignment.

My father quickly adapted to the rhythms of the White House and Washington because he excelled at networking. Dad was determined to meet everyone everywhere. I was amazed and jealous when I flipped through the two expansive rolodexes in his study. They were filled with scores of valuable and legendary political contacts. These rolodex cards contained not only the public phone numbers of his most trusted sources but also their elusive private ones as well.

These contacts included a number of people from the Kennedy White House. Dad loved dealing with Kennedy's staff members because he said they leaked like "sieves." My father also took great pride in coining the term "Irish Mafia" to describe them. Some in the Kennedy circle who started out as sources eventually became friends as well.

But Dad wasn't just infiltrating the president's administration; he was also learning how to decipher John F. Kennedy himself. And vice versa. As he would later tell the president's library, "It was typical of Kennedy that he'd say to a young reporter, 'What do you think?'"

Dad felt JFK did this for two reasons. One, he thought the president was a bit of a gossip and he liked to "kibitz" with reporters to see what they were hearing. Secondly, by asking reporters what they were thinking, Kennedy was also sizing them up, seeing how smart they were.

"Smart" may be the key word here. In one of his more candid comments to the JFK Library, my father confided, "The Kennedys are very good at courting reporters... They genuinely like reporters... If you're a dumb reporter they won't give you any time. If you're a smart reporter they'll court you." Dad even went so far as to describe the president's wooing of the press as a form of seduction.

In one of Dad's files marked simply "Letters," I came across some notes from Kennedy's father, Joseph. My father knew how much influence Kennedy Sr. had with his son and made sure he kept in contact with the family patriarch. Dad suspected JFK learned from his father the importance of taking care of the press. But oddly enough, the nation's first television president may have been a bit skeptical about exploiting the full power of the new medium. My father thought JFK was especially concerned about overexposure, even up to the time of the president's assassination.

Sorting through Dad's Kennedy papers and interviews, I was surprised to see how much pressure he felt covering the White House. This pressure came mostly from NBC, but also, I suspect, some of it was self-inflicted. He told the JFK Library the pressure was enormous and very tough on him. "In those times, God Almighty, the pressure on you on the part of your office to come up with these things all the time is murder."

This revelation surprised me. I had always had this heroic notion of my dad being in control of any situation he found himself in. To learn he was actually human, that he felt pressure about not being scooped by other reporters, was a bit eye-opening. It was also, in an odd sort of way, reassuring. Decades later, I too would feel a similar kind of pressure. I dreaded being beaten on political stories in Utah. While I think the anxiety my father and I felt made us better reporters, I've sometimes wondered if it took a bit of an emotional toll on each of us.

Being in Kennedy's good graces was very much a double-edged sword for my father. While it helped him get good stories, it also left him open to accusations that he was too close to JFK. To his credit, Dad often addressed this criticism head-on. I found this comment to the JFK Oral History Project especially insightful: "It's very interesting to listen about all these networks now, or all these newspapers, accusing that person or the other person of being very, very close to the Kennedys. Let me tell you something, that's exactly what your offices wanted. They wanted it badly because that sold newspapers and attracted viewers."

Clearly, some criticism of my father being too close to the Kennedys got under his skin. It was especially irksome when it came from Republicans. Especially one Republican in particular. In an interview decades later, Dad was pointedly asked if he was too close to the Kennedys. He gave this very direct response: "The only time the accusation about being close to the Kennedy brothers bothers me is when it's delivered by people who worked for Richard Nixon."

More on Nixon later. Much more.

But for the most part, my father patiently answered questions about his access to JFK. And those questions would pretty much dog him for the rest of his career. Here's how he summed it up for the JFK Oral History Collection: "There's always a danger [of being too close]... And whatever blame is assigned to me, I'll take responsibility. [But] I want to share some of it with the people you work for, who valued the fact that you had an in at the White House."

Which is not to say Dad wasn't tough on JFK when he needed to be. A prime example of this was his coverage of The Bay of Pigs. In April 1961, Cuban exiles launched a covert invasion of their former homeland. This mission was secretly funded and orchestrated by the U.S. government. But the botched invasion was a spectacular failure both for the United States and its new president. This led the Kennedy administration to try and dodge press questions about its international blunder. But Dad got pissed off about being stonewalled and confronted Kennedy at a presidential press conference.

In rather pointed terms, my father asked, "Sir, since last Saturday, a certain foreign policy situation has given rise to many conflicting stories. During that time, reporters in Washington have noticed that there's been a clamming up of information from formerly useful sources. To my knowledge, the State Department and the White House have not attempted to take a representative group of reporters and say, 'These are the facts as we know them.' And this morning, we are not permitted to ask any further questions about this foreign policy situation. In view of the fact we're taking a propaganda lambasting around the world, why is it not useful, sir, for us to explore with you the real facts behind this or our motivations?"

At a Bay of Pigs panel discussion years later, my father confided to the audience, "I was angry. I thought it was a stupid move and I did not like the idea that, having committed this stupidity, Kennedy would not permit any questions. Later that day, I walked into Pierre Salinger's office… and Kennedy was there. He lit into me."

This image of an angry JFK chewing out my father made me proud. Dad had held his ground and asked the popular president a tough question. That was his job as a reporter. In my mind, it also helped rebuke the notion my father had been too close to the Kennedys.

At that same panel discussion, Dad also told the audience, "After all these years, I found myself believing in one conclusion… He [JFK] deserved all the abuse he got at the time. But he got a very valuable lesson, which was not to trust the judgment of the so-called experts, civilian or military."

Decades later, I too would display some of these same outraged reporting sensibilities. When officials withheld public information from me, I also took it personally. When they lied to me or avoided me, I also responded with renewed vigor. By design or not, Dad showed me how to be dogged when pursuing a story.

But my father's coverage of the Kennedy White House also taught me another useful lesson: It's not just the politicians who have power and knowledge. Dad made it a point to stay on good terms with Kennedy's aides and even with his security team. One time, my father found and returned the lost wallet of a Secret Service agent. In return for his good deed, Dad was allowed to stake out a prime position at the 1964 Democratic Convention. This led to my father getting an exclusive and extended live interview with President Lyndon B. Johnson.

My father always strived to maintain good relationships with the families of the elected officials he covered. For example, in March of 1961, my father got an exclusive interview with First Lady Jacqueline Kennedy. While that may not sound all that significant, remember how popular Jackie Kennedy was at that time.

My father later covered Jackie Kennedy's trip to India and Pakistan in early 1962. In Dad's study, I found his battered TV scripts about her visit. I was a bit surprised to learn NBC News had actually done an entire special about her trip. This spoke volumes about the public's interest in all things Kennedy, and it reflected Dad's emergence as a star reporter and his growth as a person. Here was a young man raised in America's heartland who suddenly found himself in exotic locales on high-profile assignments. I wondered how my father handled all this sudden success and if it somehow changed him, either for better or worse.

I found a number of short scripts in Dad's study from a project called "The Kennedy Sixties." These were radio scripts from 1983, the twentieth anniversary of John F. Kennedy's assassination. There were thirty scripts, one for each day in November. All were about a minute in length.

Interestingly, one of these short Kennedy reports was devoted entirely to JFK's reported extramarital activities. In it, my father explained why he never reported on them. He said simply he didn't know about them. While there was some suspicion the president was having affairs, Dad maintained the White House press corps could never prove it.[19]

Dad expounded on the Kennedys' relationship in his interview for the JFK Oral History collection. He recalled seeing an affectionate and knowing glance the Kennedys once gave each other at some event. My father suggested this was an intimate and caring look only a married couple would give and understand. This led my father to believe that, all in all, the couple had a "reasonably happy marriage."

In one of my father's old filing cabinets, I found a rather dated copy of *Harper's Magazine*. Unexpectedly, it connected JFK, my father, and me. Dad had written one of the articles in that issue. It detailed John F. Kennedy's visit to Salt Lake City, Utah, in 1963. It was one of the best print stories Dad ever wrote. The article was entitled, "Kennedy's Voyage of Discovery."

While it touched upon Kennedy's September 1963, visits to a number of states, to me, obviously, the most intriguing part dealt with his time in Utah. According to my father, the feeling in Washington was that JFK would not be all that welcome in a conservative state like Utah. But, as is often the case with common wisdom in the nation's capital, it simply wasn't true. Dad wrote that the president was very enthusiastically greeted wherever he went in Salt Lake City and that he was "mobbed" when he arrived at the historic Hotel Utah.

Dad also wrote about how the warm welcome Kennedy received helped

19. Vanocur, "The Kennedy Sixties."

lift the president's spirits. John F. Kennedy was still grieving over the death of his premature son, Patrick Bouvier. But the overwhelming response Kennedy got during a speech at the Mormon Tabernacle seemed to wash away some of his sorrows. Dad said it was the happiest he had seen Kennedy in months. According to my father, the audience applauded for several minutes when JFK entered the Tabernacle and even gave him a standing ovation at the end. This led my father to conclude that if Kennedy "had any doubts about his reelection… they were dispelled by this trip."[20]

This article made me smile. It was nice to picture President Kennedy and my father in a place I would call home twenty years later. But Dad's article was also bittersweet. My father sadly informed the magazine's readers that he was sitting next to a *Dallas News* reporter when the reporter told his office that JFK would be visiting Texas later that year.

My father wasn't with President Kennedy in Dallas on November 22, 1963. He was on assignment elsewhere. But Dad hustled back to Washington and spent several sorrowful days reporting on Kennedy's memorial service and the transition of power.

On Google Images, I managed to find some old black and white photographs of my father reporting in the nation's capital in the days following the assassination. Several showed him standing outside in the rain reporting on the Kennedy State Funeral. The expression on his face was grim.

Because I would have just turned four, I was much too young to comprehend the enormity of the situation. But I do remember being in a toy store near our house when the news broke about JFK's death. My brother and I were quickly spirited home because of fears of chaos erupting in the streets.

It remains amazing to me now, decades after the death of John F. Kennedy, that some people still recall Dad's reporting from that time.

---

20. Vanocur, "Kennedy's Voyage."

One moment that seems to have stood out for them is when my father talked about Lyndon Johnson becoming America's new president.

In the book *Covering the Body: The Kennedy Assassination, the Media, and the Shaping of Collective Memory*, author Barbie Zelizer summed up the unforgettable imagery Dad used in his reporting. She wrote about my father standing outside the White House as JFK's rocking chair was brought out and LBJ's saddle was brought in. My dad said simply, "Power changes very quickly and very brutally in Washington."[21] Again, it was another prime example of my father using a small yet vivid detail to dramatically and effectively tell a story.

One of the few reminders of JFK's assassination I found in Dad's study was a well-worn book. Its title was simply, *A Tribute to John F. Kennedy*. It was edited by Pierre Salinger, Kennedy's press secretary, and by my father. I sensed this Kennedy book meant quite a bit to Dad and he was proud of the way it turned out.

This 162-page tribute is filled with photos of John F. Kennedy, accompanied by a number of short essays or remarks about him. Those quoted in the book were renowned and diverse: Benjamin Bradlee, Art Buchwald, Herb Caen, Murray Kempton, Norman Mailer, Ferdinand Marcos, Albert Schweitzer, Theodore White, and Robert F. Kennedy.

My father's tribute comes near the end of the book. It's only a half-page long, but I can easily envision my dad at his typewriter carefully weighing each word. He wrote how a part of all of us was buried the same day President Kennedy was laid to rest. Dad concluded his touching tribute with these words: "There is nothing more but to say—Thank you, Mister President—and—Farewell."[22]

Dad's very own copy of his book is now prominently displayed in my bookcase.

My father was thirty-five years old when President John F. Kennedy died.

---

21. Zelizer, *Covering the Body*.
22. Salinger and Vanocur, *A Tribute to John F. Kennedy*.

He was by now a network news star, married and with two young sons. But clearly an era had ended for him. He left his White House assignment in January 1964. While Dad thought Lyndon Johnson was an interesting politician to report on, being a White House correspondent just wasn't the same for him without JFK.

What my father might not have fully realized at the time, though, is that he wasn't done with the Kennedys, nor they with him. In just a few short years, he would be back on the Kennedy beat with everything that entailed, the poetic dreams as well as the heartbreaking tragedy.

In the meantime, however, my father found himself covering a new and rapidly developing political story. It would ultimately become the favorite of his entire reporting career.

Chapter Eight

Everything in Life is Political

Despite the fact my parents were once concerned about my slow development, there was one thing in life I adapted to pretty quickly: political reporting. Covering politics just came naturally to me. It was almost if I was born to do it. As I began making a name for myself in Utah's political circles, I realized there was an irregular gene in the Vanocur DNA that made us adept at covering politics. My father obviously carried this gene and, although it lay dormant for decades, so did I. There is no known cure for this condition.

But it wasn't just nature that made me a good political reporter; it was nurture, too. Over the years, Dad passed on to me many valuable tips about work and about life.

I've whittled them down to a dozen key lessons:

1. SOONER OR LATER, EVERYTHING IN LIFE IS POLITICAL.
   I think my father borrowed this phrase from George Orwell. Dad first told me this when I was pretty young, maybe still in high school. Initially, I was skeptical. I didn't want to believe politics seeped into all areas of life. So, I pushed back. I asked Dad if he really meant *everything*. He said, yes, *everything*. I thought about it for a spell and then naively asked, "But surely that doesn't apply to things like love and marriage?"

   Dad chuckled and said, "Son, especially that."

2. THE KEY TO GOOD WRITING IS KNOWING WHAT TO LEAVE OUT.
   This may be the best single piece of advice Dad gave me about being

a reporter. It took a few years for me to hone my writing skills, but I eventually figured out what he meant. Simply put, the fewer words the better. I knew I was making progress when one semi-surly boss grudgingly told me, "Well, Vanocur, nobody ever said you couldn't write." It was a bit of a backhanded compliment, but an acknowledgment of my writing chops nonetheless.

3. THE SMALL STORIES ARE OFTEN THE BEST.

I know I mentioned this earlier, but I wanted to reinforce it by sharing another example. Since covering state government was part of my political reporting portfolio, I was once assigned to cover the cutting down of the state Christmas tree. So, too early one morning, I arrived at a Salt Lake neighborhood just as state workers were about to cut down an oversized holiday tree.

Luckily, one of my closest friends was the photographer who had been assigned to shoot the story. I asked him how in the hell we were going to cover this. Immediately, he said, "Just cover it like a crime story, like they're murdering the tree."

So, we did.

I took a tongue-in-cheek approach to the story and used as many overwrought pulp fiction cliches as I could think of. Neighborhood residents watching the tree cutting were described as, "Innocent neighbors powerless to stop the cold-blooded murder." We even threw in a fake movie scream in the story just as the tree was cut down. And when the newly murdered tree made its way to the Capitol rotunda, I described how its "pine guts" spilled out onto the cold, hard, and unforgiving marble floor.

I think my bosses were genuinely frightened by the story. But one of the main anchors loved it. He said I could send this story out to stations in other cities and immediately get a dozen job offers.

Months later, much to my amusement, the piece was even nominated for an Emmy.

I'm not sure what my father's reaction to this story would have been. But it did reinforce his point that it's not always the so-called "big" stories that are the best. While many reporters might have scoffed at having to cover the cutting down of a tree, I saw it as an opportunity.

4. SOMETIMES THE BEST STORIES COME FROM THE LOSERS' LOCKER ROOM.

While at first blush this appears to be about sports, it really applies to all sorts of reporting. One of the first stories I broke in my career was about the decision to close South High School in Salt Lake City. A source tipped me off that the Salt Lake Board of Education was going to close one of its four high schools due to dwindling enrollment. And South High was the one to be shuttered at the end of the school year.

Although my news judgment was still somewhat in the developmental stage, it occurred to me that reporting on South High for its entire final year would make a great story. So, another trusted photographer and I made it a point to cover the big milestones of South High's last year. These included things like homecoming, the prom, and graduation. We told the story through the eyes of one senior, a gifted teacher, and a beloved and wise principal. Not only did we turn daily stories on these events but we even had enough footage to do a documentary called *Goodbye South High*. Thanks to the incredible photography and some expert editing, the documentary won an Emmy award. It would be my first.

Our documentary helped showcase South's admirable school spirit while dealing with an emotional and difficult year. Dad had been right. By focusing in-depth on a school that had lost its battle to stay open, we were able to capture the student's real, raw, and ultimately heartwarming emotions. We found all this in the so-called "losers' locker room." But in the eyes of viewers and many in the community, those at South High were winners.

5. THE BEST TIME TO CALL A SOURCE IS WHEN YOU DON'T WANT ANYTHING.

There's an old saying in journalism that a reporter is only as good as his or her sources. My father certainly supported this notion. As mentioned earlier, Dad tried to make contact with as many people as possible all over the country. He also did his best to stay in touch, either calling just to say hello or writing letters to congratulate them or offer condolences. This courtesy helped Dad in his journalism career and even after he stopped reporting. When my father left network news for good, his old contacts were there with much appreciated offers of employment. He watched out for them and, in many cases, they reciprocated.

Having learned from his example, I also held my sources close. Whether it was remembering their birthdays, buying them drinks, or treating them to special thank-you lunches around Christmas, I realized their story tips were what kept me in business. In return, they remembered my little gestures of appreciation and would reward me with story leads. Sometimes even years later.

6. THE BEST INTERVIEWERS LISTEN MORE THAN THEY TALK.

When I was starting out as a reporter, I used to make highly detailed lists of what questions to ask during interviews. I would then ask these questions, checking them off one by one as if completing a to-do list. But I was so determined to ask all my questions in the exact order I wrote them, I wasn't really listening to the answers. Eventually, I wised up and followed Dad's advice. I ditched the lengthy list of questions and simply started listening to each and every response. It was amazing how much I learned by paying closer attention to their words, their emotions, their silence, and their facial expressions.

I knew I was getting the hang of it when I interviewed Pulitzer Prize-winning reporter and author David Halberstam. David was a close friend of my father and happened to be visiting Salt Lake for a speaking engagement. He also graciously agreed to be a guest on my Sunday morning talk show. During a commercial break, he leaned over and told me I was pretty good at this interviewing thing. He was always very supportive of my work, and his generous compliment meant a great deal to me.

7. EVERY NOW AND THEN, YOU HAVE TO THROW A CHAIR AT WORK.

This is one piece of advice from my father I wished I had followed more closely. Now, to be clear, he wasn't actually advocating throwing a chair at work. But he strongly believed you had to occasionally let your bosses know if something was pissing you off. Otherwise, Dad reasoned, the company might start taking you for granted and take advantage of you. Judging by some of the memos and letters I found in his study, I suspected Dad successfully used this strategy to help get him raises and promotions.

Again, because of my subdued personality, I didn't really throw too many chairs. But I told one or two of my colleagues about this strategy and they subsequently used it to their advantage.

8. NEVER TRUST A REPORTER WITH A CLEAN DESK.

It's not really necessary to spend a lot of time unpacking this wry observation. Dad simply felt reporters with messy desks were more interested in chasing stories than keeping their workplaces spotless.

And having cleaned up the fascinating mess which was my father's study, I can confirm he practiced what he preached.

9. DON'T BE AFRAID TO USE SILENCE IN YOUR STORIES.
My father had no patience for anchors and reporters who talked too much. He thought they just talked because they liked to hear the sound of their own voices or wanted to prove to everyone how smart they were. Instead, Dad drilled into me the importance of using the video's natural sound to tell the story. Or, in some cases, using silence to let the story tell itself. As we shall see, he once said absolutely nothing when covering one of the biggest stories of his career.

10. LUCK IS THE RESIDUE OF DESIGN.
Over and over, my father would repeat this saying to me. He attributed it to Branch Rickey, the legendary Brooklyn Dodgers honcho who signed Jackie Robinson to break baseball's color barrier. Another way of expressing this is, as Louis Pasteur once said, "Fortune favors the prepared mind."

    Over time, this became my mantra. When working on stories, I not only envisioned how I hoped the story would play out, I also made sure I thought about what could go wrong. Having contingency plans helped save my reporting ass on many occasions. I even incorporated this preparedness philosophy into the non-news elements of my life.

11. HOLY SHIT STORIES.
Now and then, Dad would refer to a news report as a "Holy Shit Story." I'm not sure, but he may have learned this phrase from his friend Ben Bradlee, the editor of the *Washington Post*. As the "HSS" name implies, this term is reserved for the story that makes viewers say "Holy Shit"

when they see it. Little did Dad know that someday I would break a "Holy Shit Story" that would make headlines all around the world.

12. HAVING SEX AFTER SIXTY IS LIKE TRYING TO SQUEEZE AN OYSTER INTO A COIN SLOT.
    This doesn't really have anything to do with news or my father helping me become a better reporter. But ever since Dad told me this, I've been unable to erase this disturbing image from my mind. Since I don't want to suffer alone, I have now passed on this pearl of wisdom to you.

IT WASN'T JUST my father's tips that helped me become a competent political reporter. I also leaned into my work ethic and put in some serious hours on my new political beat.

Only a few weeks after I started at my new station, the annual session of the Utah legislature got underway. I attacked this new assignment with a vengeance. The embarrassment of being recently fired only served to fuel my drive.

For example…

Just before my first legislative session started, I got up very early one Saturday morning to go to the Utah State Capitol. I may or may not have been slightly hungover. An orientation session for new legislators was happening, and I thought it might be useful to introduce myself. So, bleary-eyed, I dutifully made my way over to the Capitol. I purposely didn't take a camera with me. I just wanted to say hello to the new lawmakers and let them know I was serious about covering them.

One freshman lawmaker took the time to talk to me and we immediately hit it off. He was a fan of my father and remembered Dad's reporting on the Kennedys. Eventually, this legislator became a trusted source and over the years would leak several stories to me. It reminded me of the old Woody Allen line that 80 percent of life is just showing up.

After a few months at the State Capitol, I sensed there might be a new and different way to cover Utah politics. I told John Edwards, the news director who hired me, that I was fascinated by political power. Who had it? How did they get it? What did they do with it? Eventually, this evolved into a popular segment called "Backroom Politics." In this franchise, I tried to give viewers an unvarnished look at exactly how politics worked in the state.

This led me to cause what civil rights icon John Lewis called "good trouble." To show how Republicans really made their most important decisions behind closed doors and out of the public eye, I asked Edwards if I could refuse to leave a Republican House Caucus when GOP lawmakers closed it to reporters. It was frustrating to me and others that Republicans would hold these meetings in private and make many of their key decisions with little or no transparency. Edwards said no, I couldn't refuse to leave. Instead, he ingeniously suggested I should just leave very slowly.

So, just a few days later, I put on a hidden wireless microphone and went to a GOP House caucus. When legislators quickly moved to close it, I asked the house speaker if he could explain why the public and the press had to leave. The speaker, a burly rural politician, said he didn't think he had to explain. His comment provoked a strong reaction from viewers. They didn't especially care that the press had to leave, but the appearance of the speaker thumbing his nose at the public caused an outcry. As the years went on, Utah Republican legislators did, in fact, open more of their meetings.

Another prominent backroom political story fortuitously fell into my lap. It was an example of both hard work and the residue of design.

One year, when the legislature was in session, I went to the gym after work. There, I ran into a legislator with whom I had cultivated a good working relationship. As we changed into our workout gear, he mentioned that the other reporters and I had missed a pretty big story that day. He proceeded to tell me how a bipartisan group of legislators had held a secret meeting to discuss some controversial matter dealing with public morality. I pretended to be only mildly interested. But after he finished sharing this dirt and headed out into the gym, I quickly put my work clothes back on. I called the assignment desk and said I had a pretty good exclusive and was on my way back to the station. I had just enough information to put together a short story for the late news. Our station broke the story that night, and the next day it caused a bit of a kerfuffle at the Capitol. We had peeled back the curtain and shown how lawmakers really did their business. Later it was determined the legislators had violated their own rules by holding their clandestine meeting.

And finally, one last example of backroom politics. I convinced the then House Speaker, Rob Bishop, to let me put a hidden and wireless microphone on him for the always busy last night of the legislative session. While Bishop, of course, was aware of the microphone, the other lawmakers weren't. My favorite moment was when a senior state senator came to visit Bishop about some bills that needed to be passed before midnight. To put it mildly, the senator was not happy these senate measures had been left hanging until the last night. He then proceeded to curse a blue streak at the speaker's dais. Bishop, to his credit, looked over at me and gave me a sly grin. He knew we had captured the whole exchange on our camera. Needless to say, the story was a big hit with our viewers.

Bishop, incidentally, would go on to be a congressman, representing Utah for many years in Washington. Occasionally, our paths would cross and he would just look at me and shake his head with a smile. To this day, I have no idea why he agreed to let me mic him up for the last night of the session, but it made for great TV.

Eventually, my reporting shenanigans at the legislature earned me a unique and treasured honor. One year, the lawmakers were so fed up at the press, they took an internal poll and voted on which reporter was their favorite and which one they liked the least. I'm proud to say I was voted the least favorite reporter by a wide margin. For years afterward, this distinction was printed in bold lettering on my resume. My father was especially proud of this honor and often bragged about it to his journalism pals. As for the reporter who was voted as the legislature's favorite reporter, it was drolly suggested he should sue the lawmakers for defamation of character.

But I eventually paid a steep price for my hard work.

After getting fired from my first job, I admittedly had a big chip on my shoulder. Even though my dismissal wasn't my fault, I still felt an intense desire to prove myself. So, when I started my new job, and for a long time afterward, I pushed myself even harder. I worked insane hours, including a lot of double shifts. Some work days I would anchor the morning show and then do my regular reporting shift during the day. This meant essentially working from five in the morning to six at night. Once I even remember anchoring the morning show, reporting on a big breaking story for the late afternoon news, and then emceeing a black-tie charity benefit that night.

During one particularly grueling stretch, I was working a lot of hours even by my standards. One of my more sympathetic bosses noticed how hard I was pushing myself and pulled me aside. He said, "I don't exactly know how to tell you this, but you're working too hard and too much." I thanked him for his concern but stubbornly ignored him and kept plowing straight ahead.

And then I finally snapped.

I woke up one Monday morning with an almost indescribable sense of dread and gloom. It felt like all the happiness had been sucked out of me and had been replaced with a crushing feeling of hopelessness. I was so depressed and full of despair that I couldn't even get out of bed. Any attempt to shake off these negative feelings failed miserably. Such behavior was extremely unlike me, so I called my doctor. He prescribed a low dose of Xanax. But this medication left me extremely groggy and did little to stop my downward spiral.

For several days, I barely left my bed. I had never experienced anything even remotely like this and didn't know what to do or where to turn. But by the time Thursday rolled around, I literally forced myself to go back to work. However, for the rest of week, I struggled mightily. I remember one story where I couldn't focus on the assignment at all. It took all my concentration just to keep it together.

Eventually, the dark cloud lifted and I slowly recovered. But instead of heeding this wake-up call, it wasn't long before I returned to my crazy work schedule. I was too embarrassed to tell anyone at work or any of my friends about the experience. I certainly didn't want to tell Dad.

However, I did start seeing a therapist. After a few sessions, he diagnosed me with a mild case of depression. I was neither relieved by this diagnosis nor particularly alarmed. I simply accepted it and moved forward with my life. Unless I had another debilitating attack, I figured I could go on with my normal day-to-day routine while camouflaging any smaller bouts of depression.

Only now, years later, do I understand that I had made the proverbial deal with the devil. In exchange for professional success and some monetary benefits, I had given up some of my sanity and much of my personal life. While I would go on to win the nation's top journalism awards, it would be at the expense of some of my happiness and well-being.

At the time, I really thought it was all worth it. Now, I'm not so sure.

Chapter Nine

Dad's Favorite Story

May 8, 1967, was one of the most significant days in my father's career. He was in the South working on an hour-long special for NBC News entitled, "After Civil Rights: Black Power." This special would air the following month on June 11, the four-year anniversary of John F. Kennedy's landmark speech on civil rights.

In some ways, this NBC News special was the culmination of my dad's coverage of the civil rights movement. He had started covering the movement almost immediately after joining the network. His civil rights reporting began in Little Rock, Arkansas, which had just recently seen nine Black students enroll at the then all-white Central High. Dad spent a good deal of time in Little Rock in his early NBC News days before eventually branching out into the rest of the South.

In Dad's study, I found an extensive and revealing interview he did with the Freedom Forum, a nonprofit aimed at supporting the First Amendment and journalism in general. The transcript of Dad's interview runs for more than forty pages, and a significant portion of it deals with his time covering civil rights.

Reading Dad's comments, I was surprised to learn how fearful he was covering the story in the South. He told the Forum interviewer, "What stands out in my mind during that period is why I didn't get a club in the back of my neck because, in those days, it was very tough."

But my father wasn't just concerned about his own safety. He was also worried about his NBC coworkers: "If you're driving around with a camera crew from Chicago and they brought the car from Chicago and the license plates say, 'The Land of Lincoln', that's an invitation."

Dad also said he tried to stay close to his cameramen just in case, in his words, a "redneck" started swinging a club at the camera lens.

Again, these words startled me. I had this notion of my father being pretty stoic and unflappable. Yet here he was freely admitting to being afraid of what might happen to him and his TV crew in a dangerous and unfamiliar setting. Dad also told the Forum about one particularly hair-raising experience in the South: "I was doing something in Mississippi, a white man trying to get elected sheriff… and I went to see the white deputy and he ordered me out of the county by dusk. So, I said to the cameraman and the sound man, 'Let's find some circuitous route and get out of here because this is not an idle threat.'"

But of all the alarming civil rights comments my father made in the Freedom Forum interview, one stood out to me. It came when Dad compared covering civil rights to another dangerous assignment: "Mostly, it was just sheer survival because things could get very nasty. I've told people I felt safer in Vietnam in '65 than I felt in parts of the South, though I love the South."[23]

Despite the danger my father felt, he also said he was "blessed" to have covered the civil rights story. I strongly suspect this was because of what happened on May 8, 1967. This was the day he interviewed Dr. Martin Luther King Jr.

Once, when I happened to be visiting Montecito, I noticed an intriguing post on Twitter. I believe the tweet came from George Lewis, an excellent NBC News reporter. The post contained a link to an engrossing 2013 article on the NBC News website. The headline on the article was, "King in 1967: My dream has 'turned into a nightmare.'" This web story highlighted Dad's remarkable May 8 interview with Dr. King. It also had a short video excerpt.

23. Vanocur, interview with Freedom Forum.

When I showed my father the video on my iPhone, I am not sure if he completely understood it was from his interview almost a half century earlier. He seemed more fascinated by the fact that you could watch video on a phone.

According to the NBC article, the interview with Dr. King was conducted in Atlanta's Ebenezer Baptist Church. It noted the historic church held a lot of meaning for Dr. King. Not only was he a pastor there, but his father had been too. In addition, his parents had been married there and that's where he was baptized. In April 1968, his funeral would be held there as well.

I hadn't seen the interview before and was immediately captivated by it. The producer and the camera crew with my father made an interesting choice on how to frame the exchange. Dr. King was standing on a staircase, a few steps above my father. Behind King, you could see a stained-glass window. It gave the Baptist minister an even more pious and ethereal presence.

The NBC piece described the interview as "extraordinary" and "wide-ranging." Having now watched most of it on YouTube, I can certainly attest to the accuracy of that description.

King appeared more somber and reflective in the interview than he did in the soaring speeches many of us remember. Early in the interview, King told my father the country still had significant racist elements, in the North as well as the South.

As the NBC article detailed, in 1967, Dr. King was dealing with a new generation of civil rights activists. Some of these newcomers were skeptical of King's philosophy of nonviolence. Instead, they advocated for a more confrontational approach.[24]

This was the main thrust of my father's documentary, that Dr. King suddenly was facing fresh and unexpected challenges. Dad's hour-long special began with a wide shot of the Lincoln Memorial and the subtle audio of King's "I Have a Dream" speech. As the audio of the speech faded, viewers

---

24. Franklin, "King in 1967."

then saw my father standing in front of the Lincoln Memorial. There he asked a simple yet piercing question: "What happened to the Dream?" Just moments later in the special, a fiery Stokely Carmichael is seen giving a passionate speech about Black Power and liberation.

I found myself fascinated by the notion that NBC had done (what I assumed was) a prime-time special on the sensitive issue of civil rights and race relations. And remember, this was at a time when there were only a handful of networks and very limited viewing options. For NBC to air this was both remarkable and courageous.

I also couldn't help but think about the good fortune of Dad's timing. Not only did he join NBC just as TV news was beginning its dominance, but it was also the perfect network for him. As the web article deservedly mentions, NBC had long placed an emphasis on covering the civil rights movement.

Dad told the Freedom Forum he was quite taken seeing a moral figure like Dr. King. Also, after dealing with politicians for nearly a decade, my father was impressed by the fact that King, "Never tried to lie to me or anybody else that I know."

It was admittedly thrilling for me to watch my father interview Dr. King. Not only did Dad seem slightly awed by the moral authority the civil rights leader projected, but it was also one of the few times Sander Vanocur possibly felt overmatched in an interview. I could tell Dad was working extra hard to try and phrase his probing questions in a respectful manner.

Dr. King, for his part, patiently and thoughtfully explained why racism ran so deep in America's history and psyche. One comment in particular left a deep impression on my father. It came when King told him that in Roget's Thesaurus, one would find more than a hundred synonyms for black and they were all negative. But the synonyms for white, King observed, all signified pureness and virtue.

Dad told the Freedom Forum this was a comment he would never forget.

But for me, the most important part of the interview came at roughly the twenty-minute mark. My father asked about the "I Have a Dream" speech, which had taken place four years before. King told my dad that the speech had taken place during a period of great hope for him and for many others across the nation. What came next, though, genuinely stunned me, and I wondered what went through Dad's mind when he heard Dr. King say, "That dream that I had that day has in many points turned into a nightmare." King went on to explain that he still had hope for America in the future. But he also saw many difficult days ahead.[25]

Despite Dr. King's soul-searching comment about his new "nightmare"—and my father's fearful memories of reporting in the South—Dad also tried to remain optimistic about the future of the civil rights movement.

In the Freedom Forum interview, he said, "I know of no other country in the world which could have gone through what we went through since the Supreme Court, Brown vs. Board of Education, and accomplished so much, so relatively peacefully. And I think we ought to take some pride in that and I think we ought to talk to ourselves about how fortunate we were that we had Dr. King in our midst."

But less than a year after my father interviewed him, Dr. Martin Luther King Jr. was killed. Until I saw the interview, the documentary, and my father's comments to the Freedom Forum, I never realized how much he meant to Dad. In a particularly revealing and clear-eyed answer to the Freedom Forum, he summed up his reaction to Dr. King's assassination:

"I couldn't believe Dr. King was killed. Later, as I got older, I have this dreaded sense that society finds a way to deal with martyrs or visionaries and it's not very pleasant. It's almost as if society throws up visionaries like Dr. King as martyrs to our own pettiness and meanness."

The Freedom Forum was kind enough to send me the video of its interview with my father. As Dad spoke these particularly painful words,

---

25. Vanocur, "After Civil Rights."

I could sense the emotions churning up inside him. He concluded by paraphrasing John O'Hara's quote about the passing of George Gershwin. Dad said of Martin Luther King, "I didn't want to believe that Dr. King was dead. I still don't."

A HALF CENTURY after my father's interview with Dr. King, I found myself fixated on his affection for and devotion to the civil rights story. So, one summer I decided to embark on a week-long trip through the South. My goal was to retrace my father's steps when he filmed his documentary.

I began by traveling to Little Rock, Arkansas, specifically Central High. Even though the 1957 forced segregation of the school happened before my dad began covering the area, I still wanted to see it for myself. Standing in front of this hallowed building, I tried to picture the nine brave African-American students who enrolled there all those years ago. It simultaneously seemed a lifetime ago and, sadly, more recent than many would care to admit.

Next, I drove to Natchez, Mississippi, a city and state I had never been to. Natchez was where the Forks of the Road slave market had been located, one of the biggest in the South. It's also where my father interviewed Charles Evers, the brother of slain civil rights leader Medgar Evers. This interview was part of the Black Power news special. For me, the most chilling part of the interview was when Charles Evers confessed to my father that he kept not one but two guns for his own protection.

But the highlight of my southern pilgrimage came near the end of my trip. I found myself standing in front of the Ebenezer Baptist Church, located in the Martin Luther King, Jr. National Historical Park. I had been to Atlanta years before to cover the 1996 Summer Olympics, but I had never visited the King District or the Ebenezer Church.

As I made my way into the church, the majesty of the building quickly captivated me. So much history, so much significance imbued within its humble walls. Eventually, I took a seat in one of the church pews and contemplated the civil rights struggle, Dr. King, and my father.

It was when I was seated there that I heard Dr. King's voice over a loudspeaker. I quickly recognized his words. They were from King's "Mountaintop" speech, delivered the night before he was assassinated. I listened intently and soon became lost in the moment. When I heard Dr. King say, "We, as a people, will get to the promised land," I got chills.[26] It wasn't the first time this happened to me while listening to Dr. King, and likely not the last.

When the recording ended, I sat for a moment thinking about Dr. King, his legacy, and the time my father spent with him. Then, after a spell, I slowly made my way to the exit, still a bit overwhelmed by what I had just seen and heard. But just as I was about to leave the church, I stopped. Something was holding me back. I took a few steps back and looked up. Just to my left, there it was. It was the church staircase with the stained-glass window above it. This had to be where my father interviewed Dr. King fifty years before. I spent several quiet minutes in the spot where my father stood. I wondered what it must have been like for Dad to look up at this great man and ask him about his dream.

Eventually, I left the Ebenezer Church and found a shaded area not far from where Dr. and Mrs. King are entombed. As I sat there, fittingly, I again heard Dr. King's voice. It was a recording of his "Dream" speech playing on a nearby speaker. With Dr. King's tomb behind me, I found myself asking the same question my father asked: "What happened to the Dream?"

My father's reporting earned him a lot of attention over the years. But I don't think Dad fully realized how much his civil rights coverage had touched some in the African-American community. Over the years, several have shared their thoughts with me. They remember watching NBC

---

26. King Jr., "Mountaintop" speech.

News, *The Huntley-Brinkley Report*, and my father. One African-American woman told me about an episode when she was a young girl. Her parents called her into the living room specifically to watch my father. She was told she needed to watch Dad's story because she was about to hear "the truth."

Years later, I found myself in the Southwest interviewing for a reporting job in one of America's biggest cities. When I met with one of the station's executives in his office, he immediately began telling me what my dad's reporting had meant to him. By the time he was done, this older African-American man was crying. I didn't get an offer from the station, but it was my favorite job interview of all time.

My father said the civil rights movement was both an epic and a rare story, one that didn't often come a reporter's way. He made clear to me that it was his favorite story to cover and Dr. King was his favorite interview. He said no one else even came close.

Instinctively, I understood why Dad prized this story above all others. The civil rights struggle was clearly a turning point in American history. Not to mention, all the heroic and noble protesters battling segregation made for a very compelling and visual story. But for some reason, I needed my father to tell me in his own words why this was the greatest story of his illustrious and memorable career. I wanted to hear it not in the words of a reporter but from Sander Vanocur the person.

So, after spending a long day sorting through his Montecito study, I sat down next to Dad as he watched the evening newscasts. During a commercial break, I asked him what it was specifically that made the civil rights struggle his favorite story.

My elderly father slowly turned toward me and gave me a loving look. He smiled and said simply, "It was a good cause."

Chapter Ten

My Civil Rights Story

In my thirty-plus years of reporting, I've publicly admitted to having just one bias: I hate bullies. I simply despise those who use their power to take advantage of others. And when opportunities arose to subtly level the playing field through my reporting, I had no hesitation in doing so.

Almost from the start of my political reporting, I tried to make sure the voices of those being bullied were heard. These are the people a pastor friend of mine calls the last, the least, and the lost. I just always felt a natural affinity for those in need.

One such story came early on in my career. It dealt with a public-school employee who was being professionally slighted because some superiors considered her appearance to be too dowdy. She was also disparaged for being extremely soft-spoken and shy. So, I reported on her unjust treatment, and it helped rectify a bad situation. It was by no means a groundbreaking story, but it helped someone who felt she was being unfairly pushed around.

I also did several stories about Utah's homeless situation and tried to ease their lot in life. Off duty, I helped serve several Christmas dinners at Salt Lake's shelter, alongside Ambassador Jon Huntsman and his family.

When covering the state legislature, I tried to make sure the voices of politicians weren't the only ones being heard at Utah's Capitol. I sought out those struggling economically, the disabled, and everyday Utahns who came to the Capitol seeking help. In addition, members of the state's minority communities were frequently highlighted in my reporting.

My loathing of bullies led to my own civil rights reporting. But unlike my father, I didn't focus just on the struggles of African-Americans. Instead, a fair amount of my attention and efforts centered on Utah's LGBT community.

While it may surprise those that don't live here, Utah has long had an active gay community. And while its members have faced much of the same discrimination as gays elsewhere, some of Utah's anti-gay bias has a unique religious twist. The Church of Jesus Christ of Latter-day Saints (Mormons) has not, to say the least, always made life easy for gays in Utah and in other states.

Any number of religions have opposed gay marriage, but for the LDS Church, the issue threatened one of its core tenets. Mormons place an immense and divinely inspired emphasis on families. "Traditional" families play a crucial role in their spiritual beliefs and cultural norms.

This partially explains why some Mormons look askance at those in the gay community. But politics also plays a role. Utah, the center of the Mormon universe, is a famously conservative state. The combination of a family-first faith and a heavily right-leaning population created an imperfect storm for Utah gays.

Like my father, a prominent interview may have marked the apex of my civil rights reporting on LGBT issues. However, I wasn't the one who actually did the interview. Instead, it was conducted by a very smart and brave gay friend. My small contribution was simply helping to shine a spotlight on the comments made in that interview.

In February 2009, when the Utah legislature was in session, I ran into Reed Cowan at the Utah State Capitol. Years before, Reed and I had worked together at one of Salt Lake's local TV stations. We had hit it off and were admirers of each other's work.

Reed mentioned he was working on a documentary called *8: The Mormon Proposition*. As the name implied, it was centered on the Proposition 8 movement in California. This ballot measure recognized only traditional marriages in the state while shunning gay unions. Given the Mormons' long-standing objections to gay marriage—and their not insignificant numbers in California—the LDS Church was active in trying to help this measure pass.

One of the key people Cowan interviewed for his documentary was a (very) conservative Utah Republican legislator by the name of Chris Buttars. Buttars was a prominent state senator and no friend to Utah's LGBT community. Not only did he vociferously oppose expanding civil rights for gays, but he even boasted to Cowan about personally killing legislative bills dealing with those issues.

Now, as it turns out, Cowan also ran into a number of other Utah reporters at the State Capitol on the day he interviewed Buttars. But as the documentary maker told *QSaltLake Magazine* in a June 2009, interview, "Chris Vanocur asked for the footage [of the interview]."[27]

This is true. As soon as I heard about the interview, I very much wanted to listen to it. I had a pretty strong hunch there might be a story there. Cowan went on to say in the magazine interview that he hadn't planned on releasing the footage before the documentary, but, "Chris asked."

Cowan emailed me some audio clips of the interview, and as soon as I started listening to them, my Spider-Senses exploded. Time after time, Senator Buttars made outlandish and acerbic comments about gays. Given Buttars's longstanding animus toward homosexuals, as well as the LDS Church's opposition to gay marriage, I knew I had a "Holy Shit" story on my hands. Somewhat to my disappointment, though, my bosses didn't initially seem to share my enthusiasm. While they gave me the green light to proceed, I sensed they didn't fully understand how explosive it might be.

Nevertheless, my exclusive story on Buttars's comments aired on the station's 10:00 p.m. news. The first comment I used from the interview reminded viewers of exactly how Buttars felt about those in the gay

27. Cowan, interview.

community. He told Cowan that homosexuality was a sexual perversion. He also suggested he didn't care if people were upset with that comment.

But the senator's controversial remarks didn't end there. In the interview, Buttars also said gays were mean. In fact, the senator claimed gays were, "The meanest buggers I have ever seen."

To this day, I still don't know if Buttars's use of the word "buggers" was intentional or not. My slightly amused guess is it wasn't.

In the Cowan interview, the senator asked and responded to a question of his own. Buttars asked what the morals of a gay person are. The legislator then quickly and derisively answered his own query by saying that for the gay population, anything goes.

Later in my story, I highlighted one of Buttars's other incendiary comments. It came when he compared gays to religious extremists. He argued that many Muslims are good people, but that their religion had been taken over by radicals. Buttars added that gays probably posed one of the greatest threats to America that he knew of.[28]

Reaction to my story was swift and widespread. Other Utah media outlets also reported on the senator's comments, as did several national news organizations. The next day, much to his credit, my news director actually apologized for not immediately seeing the news value of the story. This was the only time in my lengthy reporting career that a boss apologized for doubting my news judgment. For this and other respectful gestures, he remains one of my all-time favorite bosses.

Needless to say, Buttars's remarks caused quite a stir in both Utah's gay and straight communities. After much outcry both inside and outside the State Capitol building, Buttars was soon stripped of some key responsibilities at the legislature.

The senator's homophobic comments were, of course, prominently displayed in Cowan's documentary. I was quite happy for my friend when his

28. Buttars, interview.

work was selected to be shown at the Sundance Film Festival in Utah. I was proud to attend its public screening at Sundance with some LGBT friends. Reed was even kind enough to include some clips from my news reports in his film.

I don't know how, if at all, my father's coverage of civil rights in the sixties inspired me to follow a similar path. But of one thing I'm sure: I am proud of how I covered the battle for LGBT equality. I feel blessed to have been able to report on it. And if my father or anyone else were to ask me why, the answer would be simple and familiar. The LGBT cause was a good one.

And speaking of my father...

Dad made it a point at least once or twice a year to visit Utah. On one of these occasions, he treated me to dinner at an upscale Salt Lake restaurant. After our usual lengthy discussions about politics and TV news, he abruptly changed topics. After an awkward pause, he said, "So, son, how's the love life?"

Something in the way he asked this immediately caught my attention. His demeanor was a bit stilted and he appeared uncomfortable. Suddenly, a strange and unexpected thought popped into my head. Did my father think I was gay? Was he surreptitiously asking about my sexual orientation?

Because of my strong intuitive sense, and because I had consumed a couple glasses of wine, I decided to call his bluff. I asked him point-blank, "Dad, do you think I'm gay?"

The stunned and flummoxed look on his face proved I had been right about my hunch. My father was, in fact, asking about my sexual preference.

Sensing I had momentarily unnerved him, I then tried to set things straight. I calmly explained there was a reason I was still single. I told him truthfully a lot of it had to do with me being a workaholic, as well as being a non-Mormon living in Utah. These twin obstacles made it difficult for me to meet prospective brides. It wasn't, as he suspected, because I was gay.

Not that there is anything wrong with that.

(I don't mean in any way to imply here that my father was anti-gay. I think Dad would have been fine if I had told him I was. He had long been quite progressive on social issues.)

But speaking of "not that there is anything wrong with that" and Jerry Seinfeld...

I know some Utahns have also wondered from time to time about my sexual orientation. After all, I wasn't married and was reasonably sure I had no children. I was also, through my reports, supportive of Utah's gay community.

Because of all this, from time to time, I would be asked which team I played for. I often responded with yet another *Seinfeld* line: "I am not gay. I am, however, thin, single, and neat. Sometimes when someone is thin, single, and neat people assume they are gay because that is a stereotype."[29]

But putting all *Seinfeld* jokes aside, I will say this. I look back at my coverage of the LGBT community fondly. I would also like to think my stories, at least in some small way, made a difference. And while some might be critical of me or my biased coverage, I would do it all over again in a heartbeat. I have absolutely no regrets about using my "bully" pulpit to make sure the voices of Utah's gay community were heard.

29. Seinfeld, *Seinfeld*.

Chapter Eleven

Vietnam

Reed Cowan's Sundance documentary wasn't the only one that included clips of a Vanocur reporting.

Many years before, in the late 1980s, I went to see another documentary at Robert Redford's film festival in Park City, Utah. This documentary was called *Dear America: Letters Home from Vietnam*. I didn't know much about it, but it had been highly recommended by a friend. The film used prominent actors and actresses reading poignant letters written by brave soldiers who served in Vietnam. These letters were also interspersed with short news clips from the war.

Not long after *Dear America* began, suddenly my dad appeared on the screen. He was sitting on some sandbags on a Vietnamese beach. Even though it was quite late and I had already seen several other documentaries that day, I was jolted awake by his unexpected appearance. I had absolutely no clue he was in the documentary and couldn't wait to hear what he had to say.

As the camera slowly panned from a shot of military boats out on the water, it revealed a significant amount of military hardware on the sand behind my father. As he began to speak, the top of the screen read, "December 20th, 1965." On the bottom, it said simply: "Sander Vanocur, NBC News."

My thirty-seven-year-old father was wearing a khaki green shirt and holding a sheaf of papers. The wind rustled both his hair and scripts. In a very serious tone, he started his news soliloquy. He told the audience that he was at Cam Ranh Bay on the South China Sea. He also noted it was becoming a chief port of entry for American forces.

My father then turned his head slightly as he looked at the scene behind him. The background now included tanks and servicemen. Dad continued his remarks. "It is taking on a look of permanence." He also ominously predicted that there was not going to be a quick or painless way out of the war.

Then, as he looked down at his papers, the camera cut to a tighter shot of my father's face. His look was pensive. He concluded his televised comments by reporting that the possibility of 300,000 Americans in Vietnam was "now considered likely."[30]

Because I was still very young when it was filmed, I had never seen this Vietnam video before. But watching it filled me with immense pride. Not only was I proud that Dad was part of this powerful and evocative documentary, but I was also greatly moved by what he said.

The one line that fascinated me the most was, "It is taking on a look of permanence." In just this one phrase, Dad expressed so much. He was suggesting to the TV audience that what they were being told about Vietnam was, at best, wrong and, at worst, a lie. But my father did this ever so subtly. He wasn't banging his fist on some mythical international table and yelling, "This war must end!" No, instead, Dad was quietly and sadly telling anyone who cared to listen that Vietnam was, in the words of his dear friend, David Halberstam, a quagmire.

I thought this was one of the best on-camera moments of his career.

At that time, Dad had just returned to NBC News after a lengthy contract dispute. (Remember, sometimes at work you have to throw a chair.) Just as he was settling into his new role as the Washington correspondent for the *Today* show, he got some unexpected marching orders from his NBC bosses: they wanted him to go to Southeast Asia to report on the war.

But Dad didn't want to go. Part of his reluctance, I'd like to think, was because he had a family with two young sons. Also, as he later made clear in his writings, he "abhorred" physical violence, especially when it involved bullets being fired in his vicinity.

---

30. *Dear America.*

(Only a few years later, our neighbor across the street, Ted Yates, a talented NBC producer, was tragically killed in a combat zone.)

Given my father's reluctance to go to Vietnam, he pleaded his case to his bosses. But, as Dad would later explain, the vice president of NBC News told him the network wanted to send its best reporter to cover the war.

Dad was not overly impressed by this argument, but eventually decided to go. His work in Vietnam took him away from home for many weeks. Even though he was often away on business, this seemed like an especially long absence even for him. Upon his return, I remember my brother and I being overjoyed to see him. We also delighted in the Vietnamese presents we soon found in his well-worn suitcase.

In Dad's study, these Vietnam memories came rushing back. I found some old black and white photos in his files of him reporting in Southeast Asia. I was struck by how young he looked and how serious the expression was on his face.

I also unearthed many of his TV scripts from 1965, as well as his later radio reports from the seventies. Also of note were two articles about Vietnam, one written by my father and another about him. Collectively, they showed a reporter (and a person) being pulled in different, conflicting directions by the war.

On the one hand, his reports publicly praised and supported the soldiers fighting the war. He reported on their bravery and their highly valued service to our country. He also dutifully reported on a visit to Vietnam by one of the architects of the war, Secretary of Defense Robert McNamara. Among my father's Vietnam papers, there was even a highly detailed itinerary for a McNamara visit to Da Nang. It said there would be a tour of the area and transport would be provided by a C-123. I tried to imagine what it was like for Dad flying there early one morning from Saigon. Was he scared? Did he worry about being in a military plane in a war zone? If he was frightened, though, he never mentioned it to me.

In researching my father's reporting on Vietnam, I happened upon a book called *Shadows of Vietnam: Lyndon Johnson's Wars.* In it, the author tells a story about my father catching a ride back to Saigon with McNamara. Reportedly, when the defense secretary asked how he viewed the war, Dad conveyed he was a bit despondent. My father told McNamara that he was worried the U.S. forces were being spread too thin and that it seemed to be a "bottomless pit." To which the defense secretary replied, "Every pit has its bottom, Mr. Vanocur."[31]

But my father disagreed. His NBC News scripts during that time hinted at his growing skepticism of the war. Just like his comments in the *Dear America* documentary, these scripts foretold more troops, more bloodshed, and more fatalities. He ended one report saying McNamara's visit seemed to be paving the way for a massive injection of more American troops into Vietnam.

But in the two articles I found in his study, my father was even more strident and explicit in his statements about the war.

One was a dimly photocopied newspaper clip written by an Ed Perez. It doesn't say what newspaper the article ran in or when. But connecting the dots, it appears it was written after a speech Dad made at Louisiana State University (LSU) in Baton Rouge. My guess is that it's from the mid-sixties when President Johnson was still in office.

Perez quoted my father's forthright address at length. Without the time and content restrictions of his TV reports, Dad was able to add more context to his views about the war. Instead of just talking about the vast numbers of U.S. soldiers there, he could also focus on the big picture.

Perez wrote that my father felt the real stakes in Vietnam were whether America wanted to be a global police force, propping up weak governments around the world. But my father was also concerned about how other countries might respond to our increasingly aggressive approach

31. Vandiver, *Shadows of Vietnam.*

in Southeast Asia. Finally, in his LSU remarks, Dad warned of the possibility of a thermo-nuclear exchange with Red China. He feared America's involvement in Vietnam might push the Soviets and China closer together.

This southern speech also made mention of growing skepticism in the nation's capital, at least among some journalists. Dad revealed that among reporters in the Washington press corps, there was a gnawing feeling they were being used to promote the war effort. And the angst in Washington wasn't just being felt by journalists. Dad also noted, "Some Washington senators feel South Vietnam 'is not worth one soldier's life.'"[32] While I don't know for a fact which senators my father was talking about, this comment made me think about some of Dad's closer contacts in the nation's capital. These included senators like Hubert Humphrey, Robert Kennedy, Gaylord Nelson, and Abraham Ribicoff.

A number of years later, in its January 1972, issue, *Esquire* magazine printed a lengthy essay written by my father. It was called "How the Media Massaged Me." In all honesty, it's a pretty trippy piece. In it, Dad spends a lot of time talking about his frustrations with network news and what he saw as its severe limitations. After reading it, I was actually kind of worried about his state of mind back then. The piece reminded me of when Peter Finch went off the rails in the movie *Network*. It was sort of a written version of, "I'm as mad as hell, and I'm not going to take it anymore!" (As a brief sarcastic aside, Dad often said he considered *Network* to be a "training film.")

But putting aside my concerns about Dad's florid writing style in the *Esquire* article, its most lucid sections deal with Vietnam. In these, my father was not just abundantly sane but also rather profound and prescient.

One of the first things the *Esquire* article revealed was when my father first started having doubts about the Vietnam War. I had long believed his concerns began following his reporting there in 1965. But according to

---

32. Vanocur, southern speech.

this article, Dad's reservations about the conflict actually began in 1963. This, I believe, would have made him one the earliest and highest profile observers to question our policy there. His time in Vietnam merely served as an accelerant to his already existing doubts.

In the *Esquire* piece, Dad scolded President Johnson for not being upfront with the American public when it came to Vietnam. He also lamented the fact that the number of Americans fighting in Vietnam had, at one point, grown to half a million.[33] His written words reinforced what he had said on-camera in *Dear America*. My father had long known the United States would become "mired" in Vietnam.

When I finished reading the *Esquire* piece, I was struck by a rather curious thought: Did my father get the same "spidey" premonitions about news stories that I did? I couldn't help but wonder if we both had some sort of heightened reporting intuition that allowed us to anticipate big stories. After all, Dad was right early on about Vietnam. He was also ahead of his time on civil rights. And, of course, he had Richard Nixon pegged from the get-go. It had never occurred to me before, but perhaps I had inherited this arachno-ability from him.

But my father's opposition to the Vietnam War did not come as a total surprise to me. I had heard him talk about it often at home, but I was too young to understand exactly why he felt so strongly about America's involvement. I had incorrectly assumed he was opposed to the conflict solely because of his then center-left politics. However, reading his TV reports, his speeches, and the articles by and about him made me realize his anti-war stance was more complicated and layered.

In his lengthy interview with the Freedom Forum, Dad talked about his studies at the London School of Economics and how they influenced his thinking about history and international relations. He told the interviewer, "I took a bit of heavy baggage with me because of my experience

33. Vanocur, "How the Media."

in England with the French who were being forced out of Indochina, especially after Dien Bien Phu."

My father also shared an interesting anecdote related to that northwestern Vietnamese city. He told the interviewer about a visit he made to an American military base in Vietnam. Dad explained how he had a copy of a book called *La bataille de Dien Bien Phu* by Jules Roy, a French writer. But Dad said the book was taken from him at the base. He suspected it was because the book detailed France's military shortcomings in Vietnam just a few years before.

When I found out Dad had been reading it, it made me think about his time in the military. Specifically, whether my father's own service to his country influenced his thinking about Vietnam.

In a semi-hidden, rusting file cabinet near my father's study, I found his sixty-year-old military records. Dad had served as an Army intelligence officer in Berlin in the early to mid-1950s. While we never really discussed his duties there, I was able to cobble together some useful information from these files.

Upon his honorable discharge, my father received a letter from his commanding officer. The letter was addressed to "Lieutenant Vanocur." Its overall tone was highly complimentary, but one sentence in particular caught my attention. It said, "Your vast knowledge of complex military intelligence matters, your keen perception and ready solution of peculiar intelligence problems were to a great degree responsible for the success of this Detachment in Berlin."

This made me curious about what Dad's specific army duties were. He was, after all, in Berlin during the growing tensions of the Cold War. Exactly what sort of "complex military intelligence matters" was he dealing with? Could my whip-smart and sometimes secretive father actually have been some sort of spy?

My father's military intelligence background made me reexamine his sense of fatalism about Vietnam. I now realized when Dad raised questions about the number of troops in Southeast Asia, his questioning was likely coming from an informed place. His time in Berlin, I strongly suspected, helped prepare him for his later reporting in Vietnam. While he was by no means a military strategist, I wondered how much of Dad's intelligence work prepared him for sizing up the situation in Vietnam. I couldn't help but think his military background fueled some of his caution about America's involvement.

Finally, I also found myself thinking about my father's celebrated college speech, "A State of Mind." In this address, he made very clear his thoughts and concerns about armed conflict. As noted earlier, he had very serious qualms about joining the military. Even though he eventually became a highly regarded service member, I don't think he ever entirely lost his wariness of military might.

Eventually, I concluded that all of this—his European education, his own military training, and his long-standing skepticism about the use of force—must have forged his strongly held position against the Vietnam War.

Near the end of his interview with the Freedom Forum, my father was asked a rather unexpected yet fascinating question. The interviewer wanted to know if he had any regrets about his career. Tellingly, Dad pointed to his reporting from Vietnam. He said, "If I look back on anything, I wish I'd have been twice as tough on the Vietnam issue as I was."

My father never told me about these regrets, but he did share one story about his time in Vietnam. To me, this poignant memory speaks louder than any of his TV reports from Southeast Asia or any of his later comments about this conflict.

Dad was flying out of Vietnam after finishing his reporting duties. Looking out the airplane window, he watched the war-torn country slowly fading from view. As he did so, my father thought about all the tragedy and heartbreak the next few years would bring. He began to cry.

Chapter Twelve

Son of Saigon

In the late summer of 1998, I did something wildly out of character for me. I took a vacation.

I was such a workaholic; I rarely took much time off. If I did, it was usually just for a few days. I was simply wired to work and that was always my priority. Even when I did go on a short vacation, I would call my TV station to see if my services were needed. Other times, when I had a day off or even when I was sick, they would call and ask me if I could work. I almost always said yes.

Makes me sound like a fun guy to be around, doesn't it?

But in 1998, I was informed I would lose most of my accrued vacation time if I didn't use it. So, I decided to go big and not stay home. I put in for a three-week vacation. While this lengthy request did cause some grumbling from my bosses, eventually they approved it. The question then became where to go?

Coincidentally, a few days later, I ran into a good friend who was a travel agent. He was a wise and seasoned traveler who had been almost everywhere. When I asked him where I should go, he immediately said Asia. He told me many countries in that area were in a recession and my American dollars would go a long way. More importantly, he said it was a rather special part of the world and I should definitely see it. Curiously, he then predicted it would change my life.

I was skeptical about this whole life-changing prediction, but I trusted him implicitly when it came to travel. After all, he was the person who gave me the best travel advice ever. He told me the first two things to pack before any trip were patience and a sense of humor. He assured me I would need them wherever I went.

At that point in my life, I hadn't really traveled all that much outside the U.S. I had been to Mexico a few times and taken a tour across Canada when Dad was working on an extended piece for NBC. I'd also spent a year studying in Scotland, which allowed me to bum around Europe. But all these places seemed somehow safe and predictable to me. Asia felt much farther away and more like a real travel adventure. So, with my friend's help, I booked a three-week trip to Asia including stops in Hong Kong, Shanghai, Bangkok, Bali, and Ho Chi Minh City.

Not long after, I found myself on a fifteen-hour flight to Hong Kong. I arrived severely jet-lagged but instantly and endlessly fascinated. Seeing this faraway and unfamiliar land was a bit jarring but in a good way. The French have a word for this altered state: *dépaysement*. Roughly, it means a positive sense of disorientation, going somewhere new and unfamiliar to reenergize. It has long been my favorite travel expression.

In Hong Kong, I treated myself to some handmade suits and shirts. When my father was a young man in London, he fancied suits from Savile Row. Buying handmade clothes in a foreign country not only reminded me of Dad, but it also made me feel (and look) like an actual grown-up.

In Shanghai, I marveled at all the new futuristic-looking buildings. I also managed to get into a little mischief. One night during my stay there, after a few drinks in the Bund area, another American and I somehow managed to sneak into a Chinese opera. I am at a loss now about exactly why we wanted to do this, but it made for an amusing travel story.

In Bangkok, I soaked up the craziness of the city's hustle and bustle, including its hair-raising traffic. I even became a typical tourist for a moment and bought a silk robe emblazoned with a golden dragon. I hoped it would make me look like David Carradine in the classic seventies show *Kung Fu*. Instead, I ended up looking more like the *Kung Fu Panda*. Despite its kitschy style, though, the robe has become a travel keepsake, one I still have decades later.

Of all the amazing places on my itinerary, Vietnam was the country I most looked forward to visiting. Because of the war, and because of my dad's time there, I felt a powerful urge to see it for myself. A quarter century after America's military actions ended, Vietnam still held a sway over me.

In addition to patience and a sense of humor, I unknowingly packed my reporting instincts as well. No sooner had I gotten to Vietnam than I felt compelled to write about it. Given our country's history there, as well as my father's reporting, how could I not? My enthusiastic note-taking there became the first of many travel journals I would keep over the years. I also captured numerous Vietnamese images on my old but trusty Canon AE-1 (film) camera.

My scribblings there and my very amateur photography would ultimately result in my first major piece of freelance writing. After returning to Utah, I wrote a lengthy essay called "Son of Saigon." It ended up being the cover story in the November 12, 1998, issue of the *Salt Lake City Weekly*, the city's excellent alternative newspaper.

My first stop in Vietnam was at the War Remnants Museum. It was located at 28 Vo Van Tan Street in Ho Chi Minh City. That's what the city was renamed after the war. But old habits die hard. I still preferred to call it Saigon. Others did too.

I wrote in the *City Weekly* story that there was a simplicity and understated power to this museum. While the exhibits were not elaborate, nor particularly well-marked, they were unforgettable.

On display were historical photos of some of the key American actors in the Vietnam War: Johnson, McNamara, and Nixon. But the captured or discarded U.S. military weapons packed the most emotional punch. There were tanks, helicopters, M-16s, chemical grenade launchers, and the infamous Agent Orange. Before this visit, I only knew of their use and intent from the American point of view. It was sobering to get the Vietnamese perspective of their destructive and deadly force.

As I wandered around this unique museum, it was hard not to think about my father. Dad was thirty-seven years old when he visited Vietnam. Now, a third of a century later, I found myself in the same country at nearly the same age (I was thirty-eight). He had reported on America's involvement in Vietnam, and now I was reporting on his coverage of the war. Like father, like son with a bit of a meta twist.

I made it a point to stay at the legendary Continental Hotel. It was one of my dad's preferred watering holes when he visited the country. After a long, hot Saigon day, I could see my father dropping in at the Continental. There he would likely find other reporters getting the latest from military types, visiting politicians, and each other.

I found myself fascinated by the hotel's history and the old-school charm of the so-called "Grand Lady of Saigon." In my article, I described the early twentieth-century French colonial feel of the place—its cherry-stained woodwork, gray marble floors, burgundy velvet curtains, and the "dazzling Vietnamese women in long dresses."

But one hotel artifact especially captivated me. It was a newspaper article displayed prominently in the lobby. In particular, one line from the article stood out: "Guests staying here feel like they have gone back in time, *temps perdu*, as the French say."

When I looked for a translation of *temps perdu*, I found a surprising yet welcome interpretation. It translated into, "*In Search of Lost Time*." This was the title of Marcel Proust's epic multi-volume novel. It is also known as "*Remembrance of Things Past*."

Although I hadn't read this massive novel, it did strike a chord. My dad's close friend, Russell Baker, occasionally and drolly wrote about his Sisyphean efforts to read and finish Proust's lengthy work. But more to the point, the notion of searching for lost time aptly described my efforts to retrace Dad's Vietnamese steps. I was very much seeking to capture and better understand my father's time in this foreign land. The phrase "temps perdu" seemed a wonderfully apt way to describe my quest.

But being in Vietnam also brought to mind another bygone literary classic, *The Quiet American* by Graham Greene. It's a book that helped shape my father's thinking about Vietnam. I was pleasantly surprised when it resurfaced on my own trip to the country. At the time of my visit, it was still a noteworthy book in Vietnam. More than forty years after its publication, I saw children selling it on the streets of Saigon. In fact, I watched them do so from the lobby of the Continental.

The Quiet American reinforced Dad's strong feelings about the war, specifically that America did not learn from the mistakes of the French. It also appealed to him because of my father's fondness for good writing and storytelling. Growing up, our house was always filled with hundreds of books and stacks upon stacks of newspapers.

Because *The Quiet American* was so instructive and important to my father, I decided to reread it while I was there. I paused when I came to one particular sentence in the novel. It was Dad's favorite, one he repeated so often I came to learn it by heart. Greene wrote that innocence always calls "mutely for protection when we would be so much wiser to guard ourselves against it."[34] The author then went on to compare innocence to a lost leper, one wandering the world oblivious to the harm they might be causing. My father felt this one line from the book spoke volumes about America's involvement in Vietnam.

On one of my last nights in Vietnam, I had an unexpected "date" of sorts. During my stay there, I had been befriended by a young Vietnamese law student who worked at the Continental. Her name, Uyen, was enchanting to me. Much to my pleasant surprise, she asked if I wanted to have dinner. With a mischievous smile, she told me she wanted to show me her Saigon.

34. Greene, *The Quiet American*.

I met her in front of the Caravelle, another famous Vietnam hotel from the war era. The hotel was home to the Saigon bureau of NBC News and several other news outlets. It seemed a fitting place to start date night in Vietnam.

Uyen arrived on a classic-looking Vietnamese motorbike, the likes of which seemed to be everywhere. She asked if I wanted to drive. It was a generous offer but perhaps ill-conceived. I didn't have a clue how to drive one, and I found the whirlwind Vietnamese traffic to be intimidating.

After I politely declined, Uyen paused for a moment and then said she would be happy to drive. But once underway, I understood why she hesitated. On every other bike with a couple on it, the man was always driving. I feared my hesitancy to drive had shined an awkward spotlight on her.

Nevertheless, we soon arrived at a popular local dinner joint. It was the low-key kind of neighborhood place Anthony Bourdain might have approved of. It was quite informal and full of Vietnamese regulars. I still recall being a bit alarmed when our fish dinner arrived with the head still attached. I think Uyen was amused by my unsettled reaction.

After we finished eating, she suggested a late-night drink at the Caravelle's rooftop bar. I immediately seconded the idea. That bar had often been frequented by American reporters during the war. I could easily picture my father and David Halberstam being among them.

At this legendary bar, I found myself enchanted by the wonderful view of the city on a warm but pleasant night. I also enjoyed being in the company of an attractive Vietnamese woman, especially since I had spent weeks traveling around Asia on my own.

But toward the shank of the evening, I looked at Uyen and I sensed something was wrong. It was only then I realized we were being stared at by some of the other patrons at the bar. I asked Uyen why we were getting strange glances from other Vietnamese people. After a long pause, she told me being seen with an American was still somewhat frowned upon in her country. Then, after a nervous glance around, she told me it was time to go. Fittingly, I would later learn that, in Vietnamese, one translation of Uyen's name meant "not available."

Unlike my father, I shed no tears as I flew out of Vietnam. There was, after all, no escalating war when I left. Also, my time there had been both enjoyable and illuminating. However, as I headed home, I found my thoughts once again returning to *The Quiet American.* Specifically, to a poignant and philosophical question put forth in the book. The author wondered whether we all wouldn't be better off not trying to understand each other because no human will ever fully understand another. He then suggested only God might truly understand mankind. But instead of being a devout parishioner, the book's fictitious protagonist is a reporter.

This section of the book made such an impression on me, it became the second-to-last paragraph of my article. At the time, it made me think about my father and our relationship. It still does. Here's how I wrapped up my *City Weekly* story:

> *Yes, I am a reporter.*
> *Just like my father before me.*
> *In a place named Ho Chi Minh City.*
> *Which everybody still calls Saigon.*

As it turns out, my travel agent friend was right. The trip to Asia did change my life. It not only marked my first visit to this special and alluring part of the world, but it was also the first time I retraced my father's footsteps. Other Dad-centric trips would follow. As I mentioned earlier, my trip through the South was an homage to my father's civil rights reporting.

"Son of Saigon" was also the first time I wrote extensively about my travels. While the main thread was, of course, about Dad's reporting in Vietnam, my own narrative voice began to emerge as well. My personal experiences and (mild) adventures eventually became part of the story too.

The Vietnam trip also kindled my interest in photography. The *Salt Lake City Weekly* kindly ran several of my photos alongside the Vietnam article. Future pieces for that publication and others also featured my pictures. This newfound hobby taught me being behind a camera could be just as rewarding as being in front of it.

In a broader sense, my worldview also began to blossom after this trip. No longer was I only hyper-focused on Utah and breaking stories there. I was slowing coming to realize life had other tantalizing vistas to offer. Yes, age thirty-eight was a bit late to realize this. But, remember, I've always been a slow learner.

Finally, my life changed in two other profound ways after I got back from Asia. I can't honestly claim they happened because of my extended trip, but I am somewhat of a believer in karma. I'd like to think these life-altering changes happened because I brought some good karma and Asian mysticism back with me.

Just a day or so after I returned to Utah, I emceed for a charity event in Park City, Utah. At this charity gig, I met a beautiful and vivacious young woman. Before long, we started dating. Again, I probably would have met her even if I hadn't been to Asia, but coming back with a deep tan from Bali didn't hurt.

The other big event in my post-Asia life happened about two months after I got back. This change was work related. Simply put, I would break a huge and scandalous story, easily the biggest of my career. It would bring me both a modest amount of fame and even more modest riches. Again, I can't honestly say it happened because I took a long Asian vacation. But interestingly, this story did have international intrigue and profound worldwide implications. And because of its unexpected and widespread impact, I would soon no longer be known just as Sander's son.

The entrance to my father's study in Montecito, California.

Dad's neat and organized desk.

Some of my father's filing cabinets. I think they were last opened in the 19th century.

Mom and Dad's wedding picture from 1956.

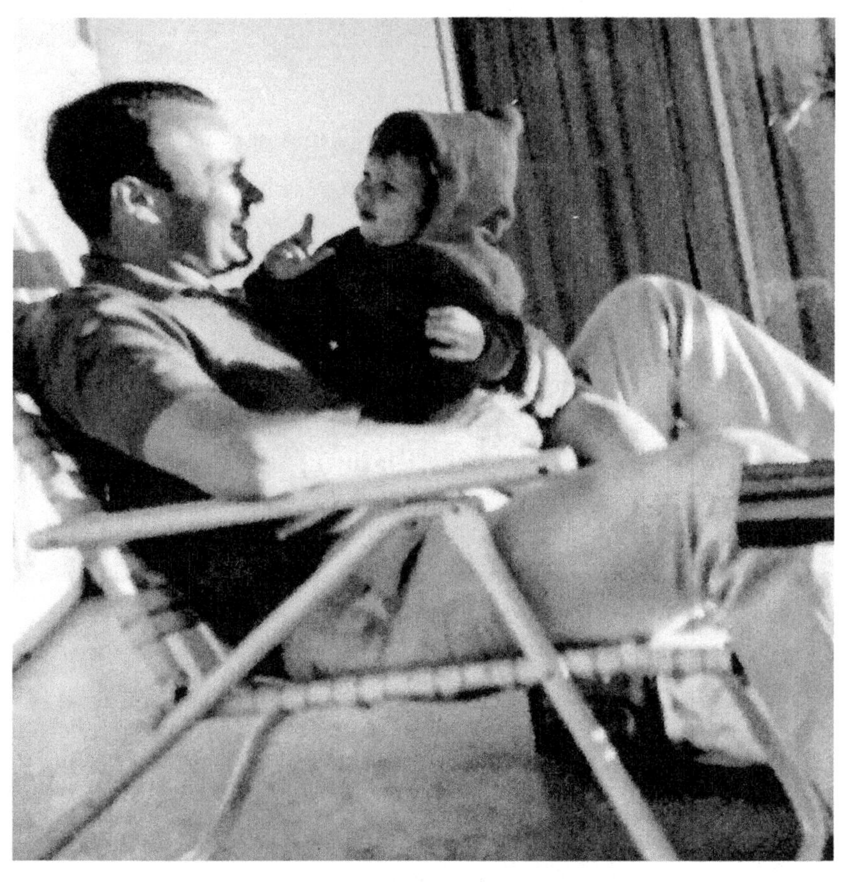

This is a picture of me asking my dad to follow my finger with his eyes.

A cigarette box from Ethel and Robert Kennedy commemorating their trip to Africa. Dad would later say this trip changed his life.

The memorial card from RFK's funeral. It was thoughtfully inscribed by his widow.

This is one of my favorite pictures of my father. The look between us is one of unconditional love.

A picture of the two of us at my stepsister's wedding.

I found this T-shirt when I was going through Dad's things. I couldn't agree more.

Chapter Thirteen

RFK

I ALWAYS ASSUMED it was nothing more than an old cigarette case. One that oddly never had any cigarettes in it. Outwardly, there wasn't much about it suggesting any great importance. It was rather small, made of Lucite, and had accumulated any number of scratches over the years. For five decades, it moved with us from house to house and from coast to coast. Eventually, it ended up in Dad's Montecito study.

There was some gold lettering on the case and a map of Africa. It had misspelled my father's name as "SANDY VAN OCUR," but the rest of the lettering hinted at its importance:

JUNE 5-16, 1966
UHURU
ETHEL AND BOB

It was only after spending several weeks in Dad's study that I was finally able to connect the dots. The cigarette case was a token of appreciation from Robert and Ethel Kennedy. It commemorated their trip to Africa in the summer of 1966 and was given to those who traveled with them.

As for Uhuru, in Swahili it means "freedom." It seemed an appropriate word for Robert Kennedy to use. In the years since his brother was assassinated, RFK had been elected a U.S. senator from New York. He was also already being talked about as a possible presidential candidate in 1968. I suspected that the lengthy journey to distant African lands had represented a bit of freedom for him. During their time overseas, the Kennedys were, perhaps, finally able to escape some of the harsh political spotlight of Washington, D.C.

As for my father, this Africa trip also represented freedom of sorts. It gave him a chance to break out of his busy Washington routine and flee the nation's capital just as the summer humidity was kicking in. And it allowed him to visit yet another unfamiliar part of the world. Tellingly, Dad would do so without his wife or his two sons in tow.

Until I started going through my father's study, I hadn't known much about this trip. I was only six at the time. But what I learned made me view my father in a rather different light. Reading about his time in Africa, and then some stopovers in Europe, I came to see this African journey as a major turning point in his life. It turns out the empty cigarette case was actually chock-full of meaning.

The key to my improved understanding was a stack of lengthy transcripts I found in my father's study. These enabled me to better understand his close yet complicated friendship with Robert Kennedy. The transcripts were, again, from a series of Oral History interviews my father had also done with the John F. Kennedy Library. They shed surprising light on the Africa trip, but also on how RFK and my dad had gotten off to a very bad start.

Just before the crucial 1960 Wisconsin Democratic primary, both Robert Kennedy and my father found themselves eating dinner (not together) at the same local haunt in Milwaukee. Senator John F. Kennedy was apparently there as well, but not present when the initial fireworks started.

The trouble began when the topic of the Catholic vote came up. Here's how Dad described it in a 1973 Oral History interview: "I said, 'Well, I understand the Catholic vote is pretty well wrapped up,' and Bobby really started to let me have it, and I got furious at him because he was saying that we were raising the Catholic issue, and I said if anybody has raised the Catholic issue you've raised the Catholic issue because you're dependent on it here. And I was livid, really livid, because I hardly knew him from Adam."

Dad then angrily left the restaurant. But outside, he ran into John Kennedy. According to the transcripts, JFK asked him how he was. Dad replied, "Madder than hell at your brother." When JFK asked why, my father responded, "Because he's giving me all this crap about us injecting the Catholic vote in the thing, and you know we just don't buy that argument."

JFK and my father then decided to walk back to the Pfister Hotel together. Here's a snippet of their conversation:

SANDER VANOCUR: You know, it's just a cheap shot.

JOHN F. KENNEDY: Forgive Bobby. He's a very blunt fellow.

SANDER VANOCUR: Well, it still isn't true.[35]

While JFK eventually calmed him down, Dad was by no means in a forgiving mood. As he later put it, "I was absolutely right because they had been using the Catholic vote, and they were going to be heavily dependent on the damn thing."

My father also had another dispiriting encounter with Robert Kennedy on the Wisconsin campaign trail. After covering a RFK stump speech for his brother, Dad was decidedly underwhelmed. He told the Oral History Project that "[Robert Kennedy] gave the worst speech I have ever heard in my life."

But a different and later encounter in the 1960 campaign showed some substantial thawing between the two men. Although, the circumstances were unusual, to say the least. In the Oral History interviews, my father described a truly bizarre meeting he had with RFK before the Democratic National Convention in Los Angeles. Dad wanted to see how the

35. Kennedy and Vanocur, interview, JFK Oral History.

California delegation was going to vote, so he visited Robert Kennedy at the Biltmore Hotel:

"It was a Saturday afternoon… I went up to his room, and he was getting undressed to take a bath so he said, 'Why don't you come into the bathroom.' So he sat there, lay there in the bath… and I started talking to him. I wouldn't say it was exactly an uncomfortable thing, but it wasn't too friendly because I didn't know what to make of him."

I don't necessarily buy Dad's assertion here. It seemed to me it would be pretty damn awkward talking to a presumably naked RFK in the bathtub. I was uncomfortable merely reading about it. But much more importantly, both men were clearly moving on from their angry confrontation in Milwaukee.

Robert Kennedy and my father would continue to cross paths over the next few years. In my father's study, I came across an unexpected letter dated November 16, 1964. It was a typed note from RFK to my dad:

Dear Sandy,

On November 22 at 9:00 A.M., Mass will be celebrated in St. Matthew's Cathedral, Washington, in memory of President Kennedy. I wanted you to know in case you might like to attend.

Sincerely,
Bob[36]

I'm not sure if my father actually went to this mass commemorating the one-year anniversary of JFK's assassination. But I suspect he did. Regardless, it was a thoughtful gesture from Robert Kennedy. In the Oral History interviews, Dad speculated on why he might have remained on RFK's radar

36. RFK note to Vanocur.

during this time period: "I think Bobby probably liked me as much for the fact that I tried to see his father twice a year as anything else, because I don't think we're really attuned spiritually or any other way in those days."

But in 1966, my father's relationship with Robert Kennedy changed dramatically. And so did my father. It changed after Dad accompanied Bobby and Ethel Kennedy to Africa. I assumed he was there solely in his role as a reporter. However, judging by what I read in the transcripts, I wondered how much of this trip was actually work. Dad's recollections dealt much more with the drinks and laughs they shared rather than politics or policy.

It was obvious from my father's comments about the trip that he and the Kennedys were forming a lasting friendship. But what wasn't so easy to discern, except possibly by me, was the dramatic effect the trip had on my father. What I read caused me to reassess exactly who my father was at that time and who he was becoming. It also made me wonder, frankly, about the strength of my parents' marriage. Specifically, whether Dad was developing a bit of a wandering eye.

The first questionable episode that caught my attention in the Oral Histories was when Dad mentioned meeting a "very, very pretty Swiss" woman while socializing on the trip. He said somewhat casually, "I was standing with my arm around this Swiss girl, just very friendly, you know, and we'd all had a marvelous time, and promised to send her some records from America."

Hmm.

At first, I shrugged off this episode as nothing more than innocent flirting. After all, my father was a handsome and successful American TV news star. It's not too much of a stretch to think attractive women would be drawn to him. But as I read on, this episode with my father became harder to dismiss. There were, in fact, numerous other references to enticing women on the trip.

After the Kennedy entourage left Africa and made its way to Greece, another item caught my attention. It happened at some high-society event. Here's how Dad described it: "Then Margot and Rudy arrived, and several of the leading dancers, and I went off with one named Monica Mason, who turned out to be a pretty good dancer, having a great time talking. Then Bobby came over and I introduced him to her."

After I got over the slight shock of my dad referring to Margot Fonteyn and Rudolf Nureyev by their first names, I began wondering about this whole swinging sixties scene. Again, my first inclination was to accept this story as nothing more than the usual cocktail circuit banter and behavior. But the next day, Dad picked up Mason and some of her dancer friends to go boating with the Kennedys. This gave me some pause. Exactly what kind of reporting assignment was this? Also, what was up with Dad and all these women who weren't his wife? And, for that matter, why was he sharing these tantalizing tidbits with the interviewer?

My suspicions were only heightened when I read more about this boating excursion. Dad seemed to be boasting a bit about his extracurricular activities: "Somebody took a picture of me surrounded by these four lovelies [the dancers] in their bikinis, and I must say I was a very happy man at that particular moment."

And then there was Rome.

The Kennedys, my father, and others were attending another social function. Dad said he was just, "Sort of standing by myself, and a beautiful broad named Luciana Pignatelli came over to ask me about Washington." The two apparently hit it off and even sat next to each other at dinner. Initially, I was perplexed by Dad's use of the word "broad." I wondered why he was suddenly talking like he was a member of the Rat Pack.

But then I started thinking about this woman named Luciana. A quick Google search confirmed what Dad had said. She was indeed stunning. However, it appears nothing untoward happened between her and my father. She decided to turn in early and alone for the evening. Dad did not.

He ended up at a discotheque where more hijinks ensued. He found a new dancing partner, a woman he identified only as "Miss Rome." My father was apparently rather taken with, as he described it, Miss Rome's "décolleté."

Reading about all these escapades again left me feeling torn. On the one hand, maybe Dad was just blowing off some steam. Like me, he had definite workaholic tendencies. But conversely, I couldn't stop thinking about all these beautiful women he had encountered. The Swiss Miss, the bikini wearing dancers, Luciana, and Miss Rome. I was curious what, if anything, might have transpired between them and my father.

Normally, I probably wouldn't have given these foreign femme fatales much thought. But knowing the scandal my father's extracurricular activities would cause just a few years later, I couldn't help but wonder if these women were the sparks before the flames.

Perhaps most telling was another comment my father made to the Kennedy Oral History Project. Summing up his feelings about the RFK Africa trip, Dad revealed, "I think that was the happiest two weeks of my life. It was a very important eye-opener for me personally about my life and everything, and very eye-opening about them [Robert and Ethel Kennedy]."

Eventually, it dawned on me what had happened to my father on this trip. He had been exposed to a very different lifestyle and rather enjoyed it. For two weeks, he had been in the company of the Kennedys, wealthy socialites, and beautiful women. He had been quasi-single, without the usual attachment of his wife and children.

Whether he fully realized it beforehand or not, Dad had become a celebrity in his own right. This meant access to all sorts of temptations—money, status, women. To a degree, I think my father found himself seduced by some of these temptations. I would be later as well, but on a much smaller scale.

My father's friendship with the Kennedys continued to blossom after their return from Africa. He became a more frequent guest at Hickory Hill,

RFK's home in Virginia. And Mom was often by his side. According to my dad, Robert Kennedy very much enjoyed her company as well.

An elegant photo album I found in Dad's study underscored the depth of their growing friendship. Bound in an attractive maroon color with gold lettering, the album contained some two dozen photos. The title on the cover read: "A DAY AT NORTH HAVEN, SEPTEMBER 2-3, 1966."

The photos showed a number of well-to-do couples mingling outside a few days before Labor Day. There were several photos of RFK relaxing poolside in a pair of longish, checkered swimming trunks. There was also a great picture of RFK completely submerged in the pool with his arms spread wide.

My parents were there too. There's even a picture of my father in his own stylish swimming apparel. Dad was then nearing his late thirties, but still cut something of a dashing figure. While I was again mildly surprised to see this kind of social interaction between the Kennedys and my father, perhaps I shouldn't have been. This was the way the power structure worked in Washington. There often was a social intermingling of politicians and members of the media. Also, this was 1966, a time when the rules of fraternization were likely laxer than they are now.

While these North Haven photos implied a certain level of coziness, Dad appeared, at times, to remain somewhat wary of it. As he told the Oral History Project, the Kennedys were "professionals in politics, they understood what other professions had to do too. And they knew very well if they leaned on you, you'd just end the friendship… They needed you more than you needed them."

In my father's files I also found a faded newspaper clip from the *Washington Post*. It was dated September 4, 1966. This would have been just after, or a continuation of, the gathering at North Haven. The *Post* ran a United Press International photo with RFK on a boat. The newspaper caption read: "Robert Kennedy waves as he and a party of 10 leave Portland, Maine, for a cruise."[37]

Also on board is my father. You can see him clearly in the UPI photo, sitting just a few feet away from the waving RFK. Although it's a little hard to tell, it seems like my father was looking straight at the camera. I found myself extremely curious about what he was thinking at that moment. I also wondered what would have been the reaction from the right wing social media had it been around in the mid-sixties. I strongly suspect Dad would have been extensively trolled and pilloried on Twitter for fraternizing with the Kennedys.

Coincidentally, it was around the same time that picture was taken that I had the honor of meeting Robert Kennedy myself. Although, as would became part of Vanocur family lore, I did not exactly rise to the occasion.

My father was consistently farsighted about introducing my brother and me to prominent politicians. He innately knew who it would be historically important for us to meet. In addition to Vice President Hubert Humphrey, I met astronaut and Senator John Glenn and, of course, Dad's lifelong friend, Senator Daniel Patrick Moynihan. During one summer vacation, I even got to meet then Senator Joe Biden. While he and my dad talked shop (politics), I was off to the side intently reading a book. But when it came time to leave, Biden made it a point to come over to me and say hello. He asked me what I was reading and we had a nice little chat. I thought this was a generous and thoughtful thing for him to do.

However, my meeting with RFK didn't go as smoothly. I must have been about seven or so at the time. Late one night, when I was already sound asleep, Dad woke me and said he wanted me to meet someone. But, as has been proven over and over again in my life, I'm not at my best when somebody awakens me from a deep slumber.

Nevertheless, Dad took me by the hand and led me down the stairs.

---

37. Newspaper clip, *The Washington Post.*

Dressed nattily in my onesie footed pajamas, I sleepily made my way to the living room. Dad took me over to one corner of the room where a gentleman was sitting slightly apart from the others. "Son," my father said, "I want you to meet Senator Robert Kennedy." I remember dutifully shaking RFK's hand and then immediately turning to my dad and asking, "Can I go back to bed now?" With that, the entire room erupted in laughter. I happened to look back at Senator Kennedy and he, thankfully, might have been laughing the hardest at my inopportune remark.

Fortunately, my father recognized much more than me what a big deal Robert Kennedy was becoming politically. In Dad's RFK files, I found several of his scripts documenting the politician's meteoric rise. In one of these reports, he described it as "The Bobby Phenomenon." He told listeners Kennedy was getting the type of attention usually reserved for a president or a movie star.

I don't know how much, if at all, RFK and my father talked about President John F. Kennedy. But I found it quite telling my father wrote in one of his reports that RFK was determined not to let the public's memory of his brother fade away. Dad also hinted at the possibility that Robert Kennedy was the natural heir to JFK's legacy.

RFK's political ambition led him to California in early June of 1968. There, he would prevail in that state's important Democratic primary. But the violent act that would befall him shocked a nation still grieving from the death of Dr. King. RFK's assassination would also be personally devastating for my father.

Dad spent much of that primary election night in Kennedy's suite at the Ambassador Hotel in Los Angeles. In fact, he was one of the last reporters to interview RFK and did so just a short time before the senator was assassinated. My father never shared much about this interview with me, except to say Roger Mudd had interviewed Kennedy after he did. Interestingly, Dad told me Mudd's interview had been much better than his and had elicited more thoughtful answers.

In my father's study, I found several photographs of him interviewing Robert Kennedy that tragic evening. The pictures were taken by photojournalist Bill Eppridge. Eppridge was the same photographer who later captured the haunting images of RFK after he was shot. These included the indelible snapshot of the senator lying on the floor with a hotel busboy kneeling beside him, trying to provide comfort. Even now, more than a half century later, it's hard for me to look at the photos of Robert Kennedy with my father and not feel tremendous sorrow.

I remember going into my parents' bedroom on the morning of either June 5 or June 6. I found my mother still in bed crying. Mom was pretty stoic and it was rare to see her shed tears. She told me what had happened. She also said Dad had tried to cheer Ethel Kennedy up by telling her about a funny quip I had made recently. Dad also briefly mentioned my attempt at humor in the RFK Oral History, referencing, "some joke my kid had told me."

Although I was quite young, and it happened a long time ago, I do vaguely remember the joke that eventually made its way to a grieving Ethel Kennedy. It happened at our new home in Washington, D.C. I was playing outside when I had my first encounter with a centipede. I must have been puzzled by this creature because one of my parents asked, "Do you know what we call something with that many legs?" To which I immediately and innocently responded, "Clumsy?" Apparently, my dad found this funny enough to repeat later at a time of great sorrow.

That's pretty much all I remember about Robert Kennedy's assassination. My father rarely talked about it with me. Perhaps the memory was just too painful. It wouldn't be until decades later that my understanding of those awful days in June 1968, would become much clearer.

Nearly a half century after RFK's assassination, I got a call from David Margolick. He was, of course, a well-respected author and journalist. He told me he was working on a story about the plane ride that carried Robert Kennedy's body from California back to the East Coast. What I didn't realize until Margolick called was that my father was one of the passengers on that plane.

Margolick's superlative article ran in the *Washington Post* in early June 2018. The timing coincided with the fiftieth anniversary of Robert Kennedy's assassination. I read the well-written and researched story with great interest.

Margolick noted that my father remained in the Kennedy hotel suite when his interview with RFK was over. Dad preferred to watch Kennedy's victory speech on TV, rather than go to the crowded hotel ballroom downstairs. But when the shooting occurred, Dad hustled into action. For much of the night, and over the next few sleepless days, he was going live, doing yeoman's work reporting on the fatal shooting of his friend.

Margolick later described the scene at the California airport where Air Force One was waiting to take the Kennedy family back east. He said my father stood by the plane reporting on what would be a sorrowful trip back home. Dad mentioned that Mrs. Martin Luther King Jr. would also be on the plane, one widow of a slain giant comforting another.

Margolick pointed out my father was one of just three reporters on Air Force One. The other two were columnists. These print reporters said little about what happened on the plane. My father, however, did report on some of what transpired. His reporting would become the subject of some controversy.

The article highlighted what my father observed on the plane. Particularly moving were Dad's thoughts about Senator Edward Kennedy. The younger Kennedy was constantly at his slain brother's side during the flight. The article described my father watching him "oscillate between grief and anger."

Margolick wrote that the scene on the plane reminded my father of an O'Neill tragedy. He quoted my father as saying that nobody on the plane wanted to talk about the future because the future seemed so bleak.

After the plane landed in New York, my father joined his NBC colleagues on the air. After several days of nearly non-stop reporting, the article noted that Dad's "rage was no easier to camouflage than his fatigue."

Margolick's piece also described an interesting exchange between NBC anchor John Chancellor and my father. Chancellor asked my dad how long it had been since he'd had any sleep. When Dad told him it had been two days, Chancellor thanked him for his good work and urged him to get some rest. Knowing my father and having been a reporter myself, I'm pretty sure he didn't want to stop reporting on the assassination. But his exhaustion was plain for all to see.

While NBC appreciated my father's reporting, others did not. Margolick described how the Kennedy clan considered this a "private" plane and the three journalists onboard were there as friends, not reporters. Margolick quoted Herb Lyon of the *Chicago Tribune*, who wrote, "Vanocur may be *persona non grata* with the Kennedys from now on."[38]

However, one of the other notable items I found in Dad's study was RFK's official memorial card. It was encased in a block of Lucite. On one side was an image of RFK. The other was filled with biographical information and some of Robert Kennedy's brilliant "extemporaneous" remarks following the assassination of Dr. King.

As I packed up Dad's memorabilia—much of which I would later send to his beloved Northwestern University—I decided to keep this particular RFK memento for myself. I did so because of my father's love for Robert Kennedy, but also because on this memorial card was a short, handwritten note from Ethel Kennedy. It read, "For Sandy, With so much love from Ethel, Christmas 1968."[39] If there been some hard feelings toward my father after his reporting about the final plane ride, I sensed time might have softened them.

Margolick ended his piece with Robert F. Kennedy being laid to rest at Arlington National Cemetery. When my father was on-air covering the

38. Margolick, "Robert F. Kennedy's Final Flight."
39. Ethel Kennedy to Vanocur, 1968.

emotional event, he intentionally chose to remain silent and not talk over the video of the service. He wanted the poignant images and the natural sound to tell the story. My father thought it may have been the longest silence ever in the history of television news. Dad later explained to me that the heartbreaking TV images spoke for themselves. Margolick added some viewers wrote in to say how much they appreciated my father not saying anything. This is what Dad meant when he told me to write with silence.

After going through my father's RFK materials, I walked down the path from his Montecito study to the main house. I wanted to ask him a question that had been on my mind. After decades of hearing Dad had been too close to the Kennedys, I always assumed critics had been referring only to his relationship with President John F. Kennedy. But after reading of his friendship with RFK, I was no longer so sure.

When I saw my father, I said to him, "I'm starting to think you were much closer to Robert Kennedy than you were to his brother." Dad said nothing but gave me a slightly incredulous look. That look could only be translated as, "Of course I was closer to Bobby." But that's not all I saw in his expression. There was also lingering sadness. Half a century later, Dad still hadn't gotten over the death of his friend.

Robert Kennedy's assassination marked the end of an era for my father. For the past eleven years, his NBC star had burned brightly. He had been at the forefront of the decade's biggest stories: JFK, civil rights, Vietnam, and now RFK's assassination. But, suddenly and unexpectedly, Dad faced an uncertain future.

He turned forty that year, and the political winds in Washington were changing. In November of 1968, Richard Nixon was elected president. Instead of his pal Robert Kennedy being in the White House, it would be Dad's archenemy. To put it mildly, my father's TV news career was about to encounter some serious headwinds and turbulence.

But not only that.

In the late 1960s and early 1970s, Dad's personal life would unravel. And a good deal of it was self-inflicted. This personal turmoil would leave lasting marks on my mother, my brother, and, yes, me as well.

I couldn't help but think my father had foreshadowed these looming troubles in a comment he made to the Kennedy Library. Specifically, the one where he summed up the Africa trip with the Kennedys: "It was a very important eye-opener for me personally about my life and everything." This comment struck me as both a prediction and a curse. While my father would gain the freedom he sought, this personal "Uhuru" would come only at a great cost.

Chapter Fourteen

A Very Confused Man

While my father was the subject of many favorable news articles, there was one magazine story he absolutely hated. In fact, I'm surprised he even kept a copy of it in his study. I also suspect he wished I had never found it.

This profile of him ran in the December 1971, edition of *Harper's Magazine*. I know he didn't like the piece because I found a letter he wrote complaining about it. As I recall, it was sent to one of the higher-ups at the magazine. And after reading the profile myself, I understood why Dad was so upset.

For starters, the article was called "Sander Vanocur: A Very Confused Man." Dad didn't like anyone questioning his intelligence, and the title suggested his current state of mind was somewhat lacking or askew. Not only that, but the article sheds a light on some of the darker moments of his life and career.

The first line of the *Harper's* piece was an eye-opener. It contained a painfully honest admission from my father. He divulged he had recently experienced a pronounced midlife crisis. As a dutiful son who idolized his dad, it was a bit unnerving for me to learn my father was human.

According to the article, this crisis started when Dad turned forty. This would have been 1968, the year Robert Kennedy was killed. Given his closeness to RFK, it didn't really surprise me Dad had lost his way. I was, however, a bit taken aback he would admit it to a prominent national magazine. Dad, like me, was a private person. He wasn't one to casually reveal personal information.

My father went on to explain he was only now beginning to emerge from his three-year crisis. He had recently left NBC's national news division after nearly fifteen years. Judging by some of the correspondence I came across in his study, it wasn't necessarily an amicable breakup. He ended up anchoring one of the local newscasts in New York City. While New York was the largest TV market in the country, I suspected my father wasn't all that happy leaving a prominent network role to go do local news.

What also became evident reading the *Harper's* profile was that Dad was burnt out. After a decade and a half of almost non-stop, around-the-clock reporting, he had (temporarily) had enough. He told the magazine the first fifteen years of his television news life were so stressful they probably equaled about thirty years of a normal life.

My own personal theory is my father had peaked early, maybe even a bit too early. He had made his name in the Kennedy-Nixon debate at the young age of thirty-two. By the time he was forty, he had covered two Kennedys, the civil rights struggle, the Vietnam War, numerous political conventions, and many other high-profile events. Most reporters would have been lucky to have covered even one of those stories. But Dad had been there for all of them, often as lead reporter. This meant a hectic decade and a half of continuous travel and unforgiving, pressure-filled deadlines. When you throw in all the speeches he gave during this period and the articles he wrote, his plate had been more than full.

In a particularly revealing comment in the article, Dad admitted to suddenly being directionless. He said it was like climbing the highest mountaintop and having no more peaks to summit. My father told *Harper's* that now there were only plateaus to walk on.[40]

To me, it seemed the proverbial double-edged sword. My father had worked tirelessly to become a top-notch reporter, one of the best in the TV news business. But having achieved this success, he was uncertain about what to do next.

---

40. Freund, "A Very Confused Man."

Again, this article was published in 1971. Dad, then age forty-three, clearly had hit pause and was taking stock. My father's life had been dominated and defined by him being a reporter. More than any other part of the *Harper's* piece, that one struck a nerve. I too had made reporting the keystone of my life.

For many years, my father had tried to balance his career and his life. Despite his punishing work schedule, he was an attentive and loving husband and father when he was home. But he was always only a phone call away from heading to his next big assignment. This is how I grew up. I just assumed it was normal for a father to not be around that much.

But one day, when I was about ten, things stopped being normal and became cataclysmic.

I remember Mom came to pick me up one afternoon from school. This was unusual. We lived close enough I would normally just walk home if the weather was nice. After I got in the car, my mother suddenly announced, "Your father has left home." Of course, with me being a bit slow, I didn't initially get it. I thought she meant Dad was just off on another assignment.

It was only later I understood what she meant. My parents had separated. Because my father would have been unhappy about me sharing this—and because, frankly, it's still a bit painful for me—I'm purposely not going to spend a lot of time writing about it. Still, to fully tell Dad's story, I do have to recount what happened, albeit briefly.

As Dad explained to *Harper's*, he'd had a "spectacular fling." But when he said "spectacular," I'm pretty sure he didn't mean it was wonderful. I think he meant it sarcastically because his high-profile fling attracted a lot of unwanted press.

Harper's was somewhat discreet by saying my father was referring to an affair with a celebrated film starlet. That star was the actress Shirley MacLaine. I'm not sure exactly how long she and my father were an item or if she was the only reason my parents split. But I do know this fling fractured our family, both short and long-term.

I remember clearly how I found out about it. After I got home from school one day, there was a small news article placed prominently on the kitchen table. Mom had cut it out and made sure I saw it. It was some sort of gossip piece, spelling out the details of my father's liaison. While I was still fairly young at that point, I finally got it. Dad was cheating on Mom. Later, my mother would tell me how he had spent hours on our front porch the day he left home. She said he sat there with bags packed and crying heavily. But after a while, he left.

My brother and I met MacLaine and spent a limited amount of time around her in New York. I neither liked nor disliked her. I was like Switzerland, neutral. She was just occasionally there. It was only when I got older that I understood the collateral damage this dalliance caused.

Eventually, their affair came to an end. But that didn't mean it wasn't still fodder for the gossip columns. One such columnist was asked by a newspaper reader why MacLaine had dropped my father. The columnist responded by writing that my father did the dropping. As he explained it, "Shirley wants her men to do what she wants to do." And as this gossip newshound made clear, Dad was much too independent to accept such an arrangement.

Dad also made clear to *Harper's* he wanted to renew his marriage. While I have scant recollections of the renewal process, I do remember one moment in particular. As part of Mom and Dad's reconciliation efforts, we held a family summit to talk about them getting back together. Again, because I was still quite young, I don't recall most of what was said. But I do remember asking what I thought was the key question. I asked Dad how we could be sure he wouldn't leave us again. I don't think my father particularly liked the question, but he answered it. He assured us he wouldn't leave again. While I wasn't thrilled it fell upon me to ask this, I was semi-proud of myself for doing so.

My parents did eventually reconcile, but the specter of Shirley still haunted us. Long after the affair ended, she occasionally reappeared in our lives. In a different Q & A newspaper column, another reader again asked about my father's celebrated fling. The columnist responded, "Vanocur and his wife don't like to talk about it." Dad was briefly quoted in the piece, responding tersely that it had already "hurt" the family enough.

Decades later, my father and I went to see *Spamalot* on Broadway. And sitting directly in front of us was MacLaine. I don't know if she saw Dad, but he noticed her and successfully did his best to try and avoid any sort of eye contact. My sense was my father came to regret many of the decisions he made during his midlife crisis.

Before moving on, though, there's one other tidbit from this era that has long fascinated me. I remember coming across an article once that romantically linked Dad with another actress, Julie Newmar. I immediately recognized the name. She had played Catwoman on the campy *Batman* TV series in the sixties.

My father never mentioned her to me, except for one curious incident. I was watching an episode of *Batman* one day in the living room when he happened to walk by. Coincidentally, it was when Newmar appeared on the screen. Dad casually mentioned as he passed by, "I dated her." He then just kept on walking. But the way he said it made me wonder if my father had hooked up with Catwoman. Quietly, I thought to myself, "Bam," "Pow," and "Bang."

Four decades after the *Harper's* piece was published, there were a few final comments from the article that have stayed with me. One was when Dad talked about his on-and-off again marriage to Mom. My father posited that all marriages in the sixties and seventies had encountered some kind of difficulty. He then confessed that his experience had been a "rough go."

Again, I could easily hear my father's tone in this comment. To me, it sounded like he had come to his senses. He had created chaos in his personal life and was waking up to the fact he needed to make amends.

It would take a while, but the family eventually coalesced. I don't know if my parents' split was one of the reasons I never got married, but I've certainly thought about it.

The final telling quote from my father comes at the very end of the article. Dad was asked to describe his feelings at this point in his life. He admitted to being a bit melancholy and even used the word "depression." But like my depression, I don't think Dad's was ultimately debilitating. His intelligence and drive helped him power through his darker moments. But I've come to believe his pessimism and sadness remained unwelcome sidekicks for the rest of his life. This was especially true in the equally troubling years that followed.

Chapter Fifteen

Enemies List

At some point in the early 1970s, I became convinced our home phone was tapped. And in my mind, there was only one explanation for all those strange noises I heard on the telephone. They were the result of my father being on President Richard Nixon's Enemies List.

This list was compiled by Nixon's henchmen in the White House. It would include hundreds of politicians, entertainers, and members of the media. In a 1971 memo, John Dean, the White House Counsel, raised the possibility of using the "federal machinery to screw our political enemies."[41] This is what happened to my father. He got royally (and presidentially) screwed.

Initially, Dad thought he was on the Enemies List because of that tough debate question he asked Nixon in 1960. But later, he wondered if it was because of his critical reporting on Vietnam. I'm not sure he ever definitively figured out why he was on the list. There was no doubt, however, that being on it negatively impacted his career and life.

In the fall of 1971, my father had gone to work for NPACT, the National Public Affairs Center for Television. NPACT was created by the Ford Foundation and the Corporation for Public Television. At NPACT, he was paired with fellow journalist Robert MacNeil. MacNeil told the *Santa Barbara News-Press* that their mission was to cover the 1972 presidential contest "in a more coherent and consistent fashion than was expected of commercial television."[42]

This new program was called *A Public Affair: Election '72*. MacNeil

41. Dean, White House Memo.
42. MacNeil to *Santa Barbara News-Press*.

described it as kind of an embryonic PBS News. But, according to the *News-Press* article, both MacNeil and my father ended up viewing the show as a disaster. Their new program about politics was ultimately torpedoed by politics itself.

The problems had actually begun several years earlier. In Dad's study, I found a copy of a White House Memo dated November 17, 1969. This would have been during Nixon's first year as president.

The memorandum was from H.R. Haldeman, Nixon's Chief of Staff. It was addressed to several members of the White House Communications team. The not-so-subtle goal of the memo was to determine which reporters should be viewed favorably or as potential enemies: "The President has asked for an updated evaluation of the network commentators. Please take all of them that regularly appear on each of the three networks and rank them as generally for us, generally objective, or generally against."[43]

Not surprisingly, my father's name was listed under the heading of "Generally Against." With that designation, the die was cast. When the new NPACT show was publicly announced, the White House declared war on Sander Vanocur.

In my father's PBS files, there was another White House Memo dated September 23, 1971. It was marked "CONFIDENTIAL EYES ONLY." It was from Jon M. Huntsman Sr., who was the White House Staff Secretary. The memo was addressed to Peter Flanigan, a presidential assistant. It was also cc'd to Haldeman and Alexander Butterfield. Butterfield was a deputy assistant to the president and also the man who revealed Nixon had a taping system in the Oval Office.

The memo starts by quoting a White House News Summary:

"Robert MacNeil and Sander Vanocur will anchor a weekly political program on Public Broadcasting in '72. It will 'try to reverse the usual focus of political reporting from the politician down to the people.'"

---

43. Haldeman, White House Memo.

The news summary also quotes my father as saying, "We have taken an institutional view of politics in the past… in a sense will be doing psychological reporting." The White House response to this quote was far from encouraging. A staffer added sarcastically, "We can hardly wait."

This confidential memo concludes by directly implicating Nixon: "The above report greatly disturbed the President who considered this the last straw. It was requested that all funds for Public Broadcasting be cut immediately. You should work this out so that the House Appropriations Committee gets the word."[44]

Coincidentally, decades later, I wound up covering Jon Huntsman Jr. when he was running to be Utah's governor. I was familiar with the White House Memo his father had sent because it had been mailed to me anonymously at the TV station. Given that Huntsman Sr. had worked for Nixon and seemed to be part of the plot to bring my father down, I was predisposed to be extra aggressive in my reporting on his son.

When Jon Jr. became governor, though, I decided to turn the other cheek and cover him fairly, impartially, and objectively. After all, that was my job. Much to my surprise, he and I ended up having a very solid and respectful relationship. This was also true of my dealings with his wife and children. To this day, I don't know if Governor (later Ambassador) Huntsman is actually aware of the September 1971, memo or his father's role in trying to torpedo my dad's career.

Two months after the Huntsman Sr. White House Memo, another "For Your Eyes Only" document was sent to Haldeman. This one was dated November 24, 1971. It came from Clay Whitehead, the Director of the White House Office of Telecommunications Policy:

"After Vanocur and MacNeil were announced in late September, we planted with the trade press the idea that their obvious liberal bias would reflect adversely on public television. We encouraged other trade journals

44. Huntsman, White House Memo.

and the general press to focus attention on the Vanocur appointment... We will quietly solicit critical articles regarding Vanocur's salary coming from public funds... and his obvious bias."[45]

For the record, Dad's NPACT salary was $85,000 and MacNeil's was $65,000 (in 1971 dollars).

Just a few days after Whitehead's memo, a negative article about my dad and his salary appeared in the *Washington Daily News*. The piece is dated Friday, November 26, 1971. The headline reads, "Vanocur's fat salary angers White House." The article quotes a congressional source as saying that the White House was livid at my father's hiring. Specifically, the Nixon team pointed to my father's criticism of the president's policies and his past association with the Kennedys.[46]

It should be noted this article was printed right next to another story whose headline read, "Nurse bitten by patient gets gangrene." And the gangrene story is right above an article about ESP putting a man in jail. Just saying.

But the *Washington Daily News* wasn't done with my father. Amongst Dad's papers, I also discovered a copy of an editorial cartoon from the same paper. The cartoon shows Dad standing next to two armed security officers. The officers are straining to carry a big black bag of cash. My father's salary, "$85,000 Per Year," is clearly imprinted on the side of the bag in big bold lettering. Dad's caricature is rubbing his hands together, apparently in eager anticipation of getting all that money.[47]

I tried picturing my father's reaction to this cartoon. While I hoped its outlandishness made him laugh, instead I strongly suspect he regarded it with both outrage and sadness.

Dad also kept an article from April 1972, from what appeared to be a broadcasting journal. This article included something that surprised and amused me. It described my father as a "balding yippie."

45. Whitehead, White House Memo.
46. Thomasson, "Vanocur's Fat Salary."
47. *Washington Daily News* cartoon about my father's salary.

A balding yippie? I had never heard Dad described this way before. While he was balding, this likely was the only time my father was described as a "yippie." When I double checked the exact meaning of "yippie," the dictionary defined it as, "A member of a radical anti-establishment group founded in the U.S. in 1967 and favoring theatrical gestures and stunts."[48]

While my father was many things, he was no Abbie Hoffman or Jerry Rubin. Nor was he a practitioner of theatrical gestures and stunts. But this balding yippie description was indicative of some of the poisoned slings and arrows directed at him during this period.

But not all the news surrounding *A Public Affair* was bad. The news program did receive occasional praise from viewers and critics. In a review published on March 8, 1972, the *Baltimore Sun* said Dad was, "Evidently setting out to prove that he is worth every dollar PBS is paying him."[49] It went on to compliment my father on his writing skills and his wry sense of humor. I thought the piece accurately described my father's strengths as a journalist and political observer. But just a few months later, the White House stepped up its attacks.

In Dad's files, I also came across a June 10, 1972, memo. This one was sent from an L. Higby, who I believe was Lawrence Higby, an assistant to Haldeman. This memorandum was for Chuck Colson, a White House advisor. It was also cc'd to Ken Clawson, the White House Deputy Director of Communications. It laid out a new battle plan for undermining my father:

"We should start now to build a public case of complaint against the activities of Vanocur on a government-subsidized network. Specifically, we should build a case by letters and protest against him with the Public Broadcasting Board and the FCC. Will you please crank this one out?"[50]

Remember, at this time, MacNeil and my father were not yet fully aware of this coordinated attack against them. The two journalists were

48. "Yippie," Oxford Languages.
49. Bachrach, "Election show has 2 pluses: Vanocur, brevity."
50. Higby, White House Memo.

still wondering if they were paranoid or if the Nixon White House was really out to get them. But eventually, they would learn the ugly truth.

On February 24, 1979, the *New York Times* ran a front-page, above-the-fold article about Nixon's war against Public Broadcasting. Dad thought this article was so important he kept several copies of it in his study.

The lede of the *Times'* article confirmed what Dad, MacNeil, and others had long suspected: Nixon's administration was trying to get rid of PBS broadcasters it considered antagonistic. The article described some of the weapons the White House used against my father and his co-anchor. These included publicizing the fact that my father and MacNeil "were receiving larger salaries than the Vice President, the Chief Justice, and other Government officials."[51]

My father would eventually leave public broadcasting, but the scars stayed with him for the rest of his life. Long after his tumultuous time there, he told the Freedom Forum he felt like he had been hit by a Mack truck. Ironically, in 1973, NPACT would win a duPont-Columbia University award for its political coverage. It's one of the top broadcasting awards in the country.

As a brief aside, I was once offered a job to be the co-anchor of a news program at a local PBS station back east. Both the prestige and the money were attractive enough that I gave the offer serious consideration. But when I called my father to ask his advice, he quickly and brusquely told me, "Don't do it." In part because of his stern and negative reaction, I turned down the job. After reading Dad's documents about his PBS days, I couldn't help but wonder if his advice to me was based on his own public broadcasting travails.

Decades after my father's battles with the Nixon administration, I told him he should be proud he was on the Enemies List. To me, it seemed a badge of honor and courage. While Dad understood that and appreciated

---

51. Brown, "Files of Nixon White House Show Bid to Control Public Broadcasting."

what I said, he remained quite bitter about what Nixon and his cronies had done to him. I didn't fully realize how much their vindictiveness harmed him until I found the transcript from the Freedom Forum interview. It was in this interview that Dad revealed the "heavy price" he paid for being on the list.

The Forum interviewer asked my father what it meant to be on the Enemies List. Dad proceeded to unload decades of pent-up rage: "I'll tell you what it meant. You felt like you were unpatriotic. And when you see later what these scumbags [the Nixon administration] tried to do to our Constitution, that's a tremendous burden to have."

But my father's wrath wasn't only directed at Nixon and his hatchet men. He also never forgot or forgave some members of the media for the way they attacked him during this time: "I then understood, as I read the newspapers about me, why people hate the press in this country, distortions, no attempt to reach me. And I'll never get over that experience."

These years marked the lowest point of Dad's long and distinguished TV career. Battling with the Nixon administration took its toll psychologically and financially. For the first time in a decade and a half, he was without a prominent and lucrative TV perch.

And my father's struggles in the early seventies would only grow exponentially. Not only was Dad suddenly out of a job, he was also beset by financial woes. Worst of all, though, his personal life was about to be upended once more. Not long after my parents reconciled, they were forced to confront some heartbreaking news. His wife, my mother, had cancer.

Chapter Sixteen

Mom

THE FILING SYSTEM in Dad's study was, to put it kindly, unpredictable. While a few files were clearly labeled and properly organized, many others proved to be mysterious adventures. Lots of random and dated papers stuffed into folders without any particular rhyme or reason. But just when I felt myself drowning in decaying, disorganized, and inconsequential paperwork, something remarkable would present itself.

For example…

In a stack of otherwise forgettable documents, I happened upon a small and dated cardboard folder. At first glance, it offered little promise. But when I opened it, something magical appeared. It was my parents' wedding photo from 1956. Not only had I not seen it before, but I hadn't known it even existed. I shudder to think how easily it might have gotten lost in a sea of extraneous papers. Of all the extraordinary things I found in Dad's study, nothing made me happier than this.

Their glamorous wedding picture had an old-school Hollywood sort of look. It was shot in black and white, giving it even more of an air of nostalgic romance. The photo was taken in Surrey County, England, just a bit south of London. My parents were holding hands outside of an official-looking building. Perhaps it was the place where they exchanged vows. But it wasn't just the mere discovery of the photo that thrilled me; it was also the way they looked at each other. Without going all Hallmark on you, it was a look of love.

Dad was twenty-eight on his wedding day. He was dressed in a dark pinstripe suit with a white shirt and an elegant polka dot tie. A dark flower was pinned to his left lapel. He appeared both dignified and debonair. Six or seven inches taller than my mother, he looked at her with a slight yet unmistakable smile.

Mom was thirty-two. Her wedding outfit was elegant yet stylish. Her background was in fashion design, and I suspected she'd designed her ensemble herself. But of particular note was the indescribable way she looked at my father. It struck me as a warm, knowing glance. While this was Dad's first marriage, it was Mom's second. When she was fairly young, she'd had a brief unsuccessful union with the son of a British military officer. The marriage didn't take and she had gotten divorced in 1954. Maybe this explains the curiously wise look she gave Dad. Mom was not only a bit older but perhaps a tad more schooled when it came to relationships. She had been down this bridal path before.

My parents had met at a party in Berlin after the war. He was a young American soldier/journalist from the Midwest who had ended up in Europe. She was an Austrian forced to flee from her home. I hadn't previously considered theirs to be a "war era" romance, but having now seen the wedding photo, I've changed my mind. War had forced them both to leave their homes and to ultimately find each other in a foreign land. Love amidst the ruins of an armed conflict.

I don't really know much more about the picture, but Dad once told me an amusing story about their wedding day. He said Mom had good-naturedly "kicked him out of bed" in the morning and told him it was time to get married.

Despite their vastly different backgrounds and nationalities, they worked well as a couple on several levels. Both were smart, resourceful, and ambitious. But even as driven and tenacious as my father was, Mom might have actually been a bit tougher and more resilient. Her sometimes steely character had been forged out of necessity, helping her survive unimaginable horrors.

In March 1938, my mother was a teenager living in Vienna. This is when the military forces of Adolph Hitler and Germany seized Austria. Just months later came Kristallnacht, "The Night of Broken Glass." In Germany, Czechoslovakia, and Austria, Jews were the targets of ferocious anti-Semitic attacks. Synagogues were burned and Jewish businesses were decimated. Dozens were killed and thousands were rounded up and sent to concentration camps.

These atrocities sparked international outrage. England relaxed its immigration laws and offered sanctuary to endangered Jewish children from Europe. This rescue and relief effort became known as the Kindertransport. Over the next year and a half, some ten thousand of these children fled to the British Isles—Jewish boys and girls seeking shelter and safety.

My mother, Edith Pick, was one of these "Children of 1939." That year, her father, Josef Pick, signed a heartbreaking document that (translated) read:

"I authorize the Movement for the Care of Children from Germany, to take all steps which are considered necessary for the well-being of my child in England. I recognize the Movement as the legal guardian of my child and declare myself in agreement with all decisions made by the Movement from now until the time my child and I are reunited."

Mom arrived in England on June 15, 1939. While she had managed to escape the clutches of Hitler, she did not have an easy go of it in her new country. She was sent to live with an English foster family, but, according to records from that time, my mother was "very unhappy." After all, she was only fifteen, had suddenly been separated from her parents, and hurriedly sent to live in an unfamiliar country. It made me immensely sad to even think about it. Eventually, though, her resolute Austrian resolve kicked in, enabling her to survive the horrors and anguish of World War II. But the fates would not be as kind to her parents.

For much of my life, I had no idea about the anguish my mother went through as a teenager. She never mentioned her trauma to me and our house contained no hints of what happened. If I asked about my maternal grandparents, I was simply told they had passed away and no additional information was offered.

It wasn't until early in my reporting career that I slowly began piecing together what had happened. Fittingly, it was my father who lit the spark that caused me to delve deeply into my family's past. In 1989, Dad mailed me a lengthy article from the *Washington Post*. It was about the fiftieth anniversary of the Kindertransport.

A large black and white photograph accompanied the article. It showed a Jewish teenage girl who was part of the Kindertransport. She was seated on some steps, her head resting in her hand as she leaned against a wall. She looked overcome by the enormity of what had happened to her. The identification number 247 hung by her side. Dad sent a short note attached to the article. It said simply, "I think this may be Mom." And with that, I launched a multi-year investigation into the Kindertransport, the Holocaust, and exactly what happened to my mother and her parents. I don't know if Dad intended for me to undertake such a massive research effort when he sent the article. But the way I was wired—both as a reporter and a person—compelled me to seek the full story.

Shortly after getting the newspaper clip, I wrote a letter to a Jewish relief organization in London. I requested any information it might have about my mother and her family. Before long, a large packet arrived from overseas. It contained a number of documents in both English and German. They told the story of my mother's journey from Austria to England. Of particular interest to me was a copy of her transport card. In addition to some information about her parents, the card also had a picture of Mom as a fifteen-year-old girl. It was a bittersweet reminder of her, one I have looked at often.

The information from the Jewish relief group answered a number of key questions. Specifically, about how and when Mom found a safe haven in

England. It also answered Dad's question. No, the teenager in the *Post* picture wasn't my mother, although there was a certain resemblance. But what the helpful packet from England didn't tell me is what happened to her parents, my grandparents. And that's when my reporting instincts really took over.

I approached The Church of Jesus Christ of Latter-day Saints (Mormons). Given its extensive genealogical records, I asked the LDS Church if it would be interested in helping me find out what happened to my grandparents. With an assist from some LDS officials I had become friendly with, my request was soon granted. Shortly thereafter, LDS genealogy researchers unearthed long-lost and vital information about my mother's side of the family.

I then took that information to the American Red Cross, which has long helped people like me trace relatives swept up by the Holocaust. Eventually, the Red Cross managed to retrieve the final, key documents that had stubbornly eluded me. These documents showed my grandparents had first been sent to the Theresienstadt Concentration Camp in Czechoslovakia. Then, not long before the war ended, they were taken to Auschwitz on Transports #1366 and #1367. This is where the paper trail and their lives ended.

As a way of honoring my mother and my grandparents, I later visited both Berlin and Auschwitz. While I ended up liking Berlin more than I had anticipated, Auschwitz left me emotionally numb. After I got home, I wrote another long article for the *Salt Lake City Weekly* about my family's Holocaust experiences.

I also did several TV news stories about what had happened to my mother's family. The most moving of these was about the opening of the Holocaust Museum in Washington, D.C. It just so happened that a generous museum donor lived in Utah. He had donated a considerable amount of money to help get it built. I traveled back east to chronicle the museum's opening and his sizable contribution. But I also crafted a more personal news story, which would become my one of my all-time favorites.

This story was about the powerful and unexpected reaction I had seeing the museum. I was so moved by my visit there, I decided to write the story as if I were writing a letter to my mother. The first line of the story was, "Dear Mom." I then told her how much the museum had impacted me and how it strengthened our bond.

The story ended up winning an Emmy award for its writing. While that recognition was greatly appreciated, an even more memorable reaction came from my father. After the story aired in Utah, I sent him a copy to watch. But I didn't know how he would respond. Part of my trepidation came from the fact Dad was part of the story. I had interviewed him when I was in Washington covering the opening of the museum. His on-camera comments, not unsurprisingly, were excellent and added greatly to the story's success. Still, I didn't know how he would react to actually seeing the completed piece.

After watching the tape, Dad called me at home one night. He began by reminding me I had broken one of the aforementioned cardinal rules of journalism: I'd made myself part of the story. However, his tone wasn't scolding; it was affectionate. He then he told me much he loved the piece, especially the last shot of my glasses resting on the finished letter. I had ended the story and the letter to my mom with the words, "Your youngest son, Chris." I could tell by Dad's emotional tone he had been crying.

Not long after their 1956 wedding photo was taken, Mom and Dad headed to the United States. They moved first to New York City, coinciding with my father's abbreviated tenure with the *Times*. This was where my brother, Nick, was born. Then, when Dad went to work for NBC, they all moved to Chicago. I came along in early November of 1959. But we weren't there long. Washington, D.C., beckoned a year or so later and this was where both of my parents' careers blossomed.

Dad, of course, became a network news fixture. But Mom also had a celebrated run as a media cook. She co-authored two colorfully and wonderfully illustrated cookbooks. One was called *HORS D'OEUVRE*, and the other, *BOOZE*. The latter is proudly displayed on my modest but well-stocked bar. Mom later wrote a third cookbook. This was one called *A Chicken in Every Pot*. It was comprised entirely of recipes on how to cook chicken. My father, brother, and I were the guinea pigs (to mix culinary metaphors). Every night for several months, everything we ate was simultaneously delicious but also fowl.

However, Mom's culinary skills weren't limited to books. In addition, she wrote a food column for the *Washington Post*. She also appeared on a cooking segment for the *Today* show. These TV spots were called, appropriately enough, the "Capitol Cook." Of all her food masterpieces, my favorites were her desserts, often inspired by European treats from her childhood. In short, Mom ended up establishing her own well-deserved identity in Washington.

But sadly, both Mom's burgeoning career and her too young life were cut short.

In the early seventies, my mother was diagnosed with stomach cancer. She waged a lengthy and brave battle against it, but it was a fierce and persistent opponent. I still recall one particularly long and brutal surgery in which a massive section of the tumor had to be removed. Mom steadily lost weight during her lengthy ordeal, and the chemotherapy caused her hair to fall out. But despite the near constant pain and discomfort, she soldiered on as best she could.

I remember visiting her in the hospital as the end drew near. Luckily, she felt a bit better that day and was in relatively good spirits. We both found comfort in this final visit. Dad told me later Mom had said, "We did a good job raising Chris." To this day, I remember those words fondly and longingly.

Not long after that visit, Dad came to pick me up one day after lacrosse practice. I knew something was wrong because he was usually at work at that time of day. When I got in the car, he told me Mom was dying and likely only had a few days left. I was grateful he had come to pick me up and tell me in person. It helped soften the impact of what was to come.

Unfortunately, Dad's warning came true not long after. Mom died in

April 1975, at the age of fifty-one. I was fifteen, the same age she was when she said goodbye to her parents.

For some reason, the day after she died, I thought it was important I go to school as usual. I remember having a Spanish test and getting an "A" on it. Perhaps I wanted to prove to myself and others I could be as tough and resilient as my mother.

Dad really stepped up for Mom during her long and anguishing struggle. He spent a lot of time with her at the hospital, providing as much comfort as he could. After her passing, he held an extended wake for her at our house. Many family friends came by, filling the home with food and much appreciated support.

For the next few months, my father was alone raising his two sons. And after my brother went off to college in the fall, it was just Dad and me. As time went by, some of his deep emotional wounds began to heal.

I remember one night when I was asleep, Dad came into my room and turned on the light. He then asked if I was awake. Groggily, I said no. But nevertheless, he persisted. He sat down in a chair across from my bed and told me he had met someone. However, he wasn't sure if he wanted to settle down just yet. I eventually went back to sleep, convinced a second marriage wasn't imminent.

The next day, though, my father showed up with the woman he had been seeing. She was kind enough to have brought dinner for us. At that point, I intuitively knew what was going to happen. This was going to be my stepmother. They were wed that December and their marriage would endure for more than forty years.

While most of this book is about my remarkable father, I was blessed to have had a marvelous mother as well. The wedding photo and other treasured pictures I found in Dad's study reminded me of her greatness, her strength, and the love we shared. But I simply didn't get enough time with her. I never got to ask her about the Kindertransport, the Holocaust, or losing her parents. Nor was I old enough to absorb any valuable cooking lessons she might have imparted. I try not to have too many regrets about how my life has unfolded, but this is at the top of the list. I wish Mom had been around longer and I could have gotten to know her better.

Chapter Seventeen

Dad's Wilderness Years

THE YEARS 1972–75 were the proverbial worst of times for my father. In addition to Mom's lengthy illness and ultimate death, Dad's professional woes continued. After he left NPACT, he was unable to land a TV job. I don't know if he was actually blacklisted for being on the "Enemies List," but my father had no doubt. He later told the *Santa Barbara News-Press* that Nixon had destroyed his reputation. Dad also added that it was one of the low points in his life and he remained quite angry about it.

Luckily, Dad's friends came to his rescue. During his network news days, my father had filled his giant rolodexes with the names of trusted and loyal contacts. Many of them were so-called "heavy hitters" in politics and business. And during Dad's wilderness years—when he was off TV and hustling for work—these friends threw him a lifeline. Actually, several.

One of these lifelines came from Duke University. Every week, my father would fly down to North Carolina to teach a special communications class. Dad was forever grateful to those at Duke for giving him this opportunity. Coincidentally, when it came time for me to decide where to go to college, Duke narrowly lost out to Northwestern. Had I known how brutally cold Chicago winters were, I might have headed south instead.

I do recall an unusual story Dad told about teaching at Duke. One of his students submitted a paper about television written entirely on a roll of toilet paper. The suggestion, I guess, was that TV was crap. My father told me he wasn't too happy about the choice of writing paper, and I don't think this poor student got a very high grade on his roll. Dad had a sense of humor, but I suspect he wasn't amused at the prospect of unrolling the paper to read it.

My father would also jet off to Chicago on a regular basis. A contact there had arranged for him to talk to business and advertising executives about the media and current events. This was a much appreciated and a badly needed source of income for my father.

Dad also continued to give speeches during his exile from TV. Even though he wasn't reporting at the time, he was still a well-known public figure, as well as an excellent speaker. While these side hustles weren't as lucrative as his TV jobs, my father was able to piece together a living.

When he was a young man, my father had seen one of the early productions of *Death of a Salesman*. Because of this memorable experience, he borrowed one of the drama's more famous lines to describe his underemployed status. He would often say that he was out there on his own, armed only with "a smile and a shoeshine."[52]

While Dad was able to eke out a living, money woes continued to dog him. Paying for separate residences in New York and Washington, among many other expenses, had plunged him into debt. Being forced off TV didn't help.

During one particularly bleak financial stretch, I offered to give Dad a thousand dollars of my savings to help out (I was frugal even at an early age). He grudgingly accepted the offer, even though I sensed he was hesitant to do so. Just a few days later, he not only paid me back in full, but he also gave me an extra hundred dollars in interest as a thank you. While our family certainly had its share of dysfunctional moments, the loving bond between my father and me was unshakable. After all that he had given me, and would give me in the future, I was happy to raid the piggy bank for him.

Fortunately, in the spring of 1975, another friend came to the rescue.

---

52. Miller, *Death of a Salesman.*

Ben Bradlee, the legendary *Washington Post* editor, presented Dad with an unexpected and wonderful opportunity. He wanted my father to be the paper's TV critic. My father eagerly accepted. Dad would later say that he wanted to leave his sons his good name and reputation. I was fascinated and touched when I found this particular comment in his study. Dad never let on that his legacy mattered to him. Nor did I realize he wanted his sons to carry it forward.

While my father's newspaper salary may have been less than what he earned on TV, it was still a steady paycheck and a fairly high-profile gig. In Washington, as Dad was well aware, a prominent title was crucial. Without one, it was tough to get calls returned.

But the *Washington Post* gig was about more than money. It was also the beginning of Dad's journalism comeback tour. Once again, he was reporting and doing so for a first-rate media outlet. He told the *Santa Barbara News-Press* how much fun it was working at the *Post*, how it was like going to summer camp. My father expressed his gratitude to Bradlee for providing a badly needed helping hand.

There was also, perhaps, a bit of irony attached to Dad's new job. One of his favorite sayings was, "A critic is someone who comes down from the mountaintop after the battle and shoots the survivors." Regardless of the situation, it always seemed like my father could conjure up an appropriate or clever turn of phrase.

All in all, my father had an enjoyable two-year run at the *Post*. He liked covering TV and was good at it. I still can vividly picture him ringing up the *Post* and dictating his columns over the phone. But, not unlike Al Pacino in *The Godfather Part III*, just when my dad thought he might be out of TV news for good, it pulled him back in.

In 1977, ABC News and its president, Roone Arledge, came calling. Although Dad still had some time left on his *Post* contract, Bradlee let him out of his remaining obligation. Bradlee told my dad he was meant to be on TV. My father's trying ordeal had come to an end. His wilderness days were over.

At first, Dad was assigned to be an ABC vice president in charge of political and investigative news. But it wasn't a good hierarchical fit. As my father liked to say, he couldn't organize a two-car funeral procession.

Eventually, Dad returned to his TV roots at ABC. He once again found himself covering politics. It was where he belonged. This new/old assignment even led to him moderating the 1984 Vice Presidential Debate. His resurrected high-profile status allowed my father to square up his debts and regain a more solid financial footing. Sander Vanocur finally had restored his good name.

Dad would then go on to serve as ABC's Chief Diplomatic Correspondent. This allowed him to travel around the world and also, in a sense, back in time. His journalism career had begun with his 1951 essay for the *Sunday Observer*, "Two World Powers." In it, he warned of the growing Soviet threat. Some four decades later as a top network reporter, Dad himself traveled to Russia. His time there resulted in a special, multi-part series for the evening news.

In a curious twist of fate, Dad's side of the family had actually emigrated from Russia decades before. And when I traveled there in the 1990s to file my own reports, this lineage came in handy. I was traveling with a large group of Utahns on a humanitarian mission when we landed in Moscow. The Russian customs officials seemed particularly wary of this group of Americans, and the entry process dragged on and on. But when I showed a Russian inspector my passport, he looked at me and said, "Vanocur. Is Russian name?" I said yes and he immediately waved me through. Other members of the Utah entourage, especially those still waiting in a long line to get in, shot me an envious look.

One of Dad's other diplomatic triumphs at ABC came when he was sent to Argentina to cover the Falkland Islands War in 1982. It ended up being one of his favorite assignments for the network. Given his own time in the military, as well as his Vietnam reporting, Dad was no stranger to covering armed conflicts. His coverage of the war was well received at home. I remember a glowing newspaper review about his reporting. It praised his efforts for handily "outshining" the competition. Dad was grateful for those kind words and kept the review framed in his study.

Near the end of Dad's fifteen-year tenure at ABC, he became the host of a weekend program called *Business World*. He greatly enjoyed covering the financial world, and this assignment would pay big dividends down the road. He and my stepmother also enjoyed spending part of each week in New York. The only downside, as far as I was concerned, was that he occasionally gave me bad advice about which stocks to buy.

But while Dad prospered during his decade and a half run at ABC, the media landscape had changed dramatically since his heyday in the 1960s. There were many more TV reporters, news channels, and ways for people to get information. It was simply harder for my dad's work to stand out and get noticed. I always sensed that was a frustrating reality for him to accept.

My father continued to work for ABC until the early 1990s. But, as I would also find out later for myself, being a TV news reporter takes a toll on you. After thirty-five years of crushing deadlines and endless internal politics, I think Dad had had enough. He and my stepmother sold their Georgetown home in Washington and headed west. They put down new roots in Montecito, California. Some three decades after Dad had discovered the Santa Barbara area while covering the 1960 campaign, he returned to an area he described as being like "heaven."

My father kept busy during his California, post-retirement career. He became the host of a History Channel program called *Movies in Time*. On this show, he introduced various historical movies and then interviewed experts about them. I happened to be visiting New York when he taped a show about the film *All the President's Men*. This was one of my favorite movies, one I occasionally rewatched to pick up reporting tips about covering big stories.

When Dad found out I was going to be in New York when they were taping the Watergate show, he kindly invited me to watch. His guest that day was his longtime pal, Ben Bradlee. To be able to watch these two legends talk about the movie and journalism was a thrill. To this day, Bradlee's memoir, *A Good Life*, has a high-profile spot on my bookshelf. He even generously took time to inscribe it. He wrote, "For Chris Vanocur. A good life begins with a good father, right?"[53]

Yes, Mr. Bradlee, it sure does.

Another of Dad's contacts also helped him secure a spot on the board of directors of a large mutual fund. I suspect his time hosting *Business World* helped seal the deal. This extra income gave my father a soft financial landing in retirement. He greatly enjoyed flying back east for the monthly meetings, and they helped satiate his ever-curious mind.

Still, I got the sense my father occasionally missed being a reporter. He kept up his daily routine of reading several national newspapers and scores of magazines. And when five o'clock rolled around, he would fix himself a little cocktail and plop himself down in front of the TV. There, he would watch Santa Barbara's local news as well as the national broadcasts. Sometimes, when I watched with him, I was greatly entertained by his running commentary and critiques.

In Dad's periodic speeches during these years, the media was often a familiar and frequent topic. In his study, I found a speech entitled, "Can Democracy Survive the Mass Media?" In it, my father pointed out what he thought were TV's greatest sins—too much punditry and too little actual reporting. One of his better lines was referring to cable news as a twenty-four-hour a day "Tower of Babble." He also likened the never-ending news cycle to an electronic tapeworm which constantly had to be fed.

53. Bradlee to Vanocur, C.

Dad also warned about how the media's ills adversely impacted society. Presciently, he predicted in the early 2000s that the overcharged debates among TV's talking heads would lead to further partisan rancor in the country.[54] Sadly, his prediction would come true.

But just as my father was exiting the TV news stage, I was bolstering my own credentials. Just a few years after Dad left ABC, I caught the biggest break of my career. It would dramatically change the arc of my life, professionally and personally. It also allowed me to carry on my father's good name.

54. Vanocur, speech.

Chapter Eighteen

The Son Also Rises

In late November 1998, I got lucky in a bar. But not with a woman. Instead, I scored the story of a lifetime. The bar was called the Green Street Social Club. It was one of the more popular watering holes in Utah's alcohol-challenged capital. On weekends, it drew big crowds seeking spirits and other various secular sins.

But when I walked into Green Street that wintry weekday afternoon, the bar was pretty much deserted. It was a quarter to three and no one was there but the waitstaff and me. I sat down at a table in the back and bided my time. Before long, I had company. Not much was said as a single piece of paper was slid to me over the long wooden table. We then left separately to avoid detection.

I was thirty-nine years old at the time and at a bit of a crossroads. I had become a solid and dependable reporter, but still in the same smallish TV market where I started. I could be relied on to crank out semi-professional yet unspectacular stories. But after nearly two decades as a local TV reporter, my career had stalled. I had even toyed with the idea of leaving journalism, but Dad persuaded me to give it a few more years. Had my career continued to play out at the same slow space, there wouldn't have been much to write about in this book. At least, not with regards to my career. But that single piece of paper changed my narrative.

At first glance, the sheet of paper wasn't much to look at. It appeared to be a hastily copied, crude replica of a letter. There were only about a hundred or so words on it. Most were typed, a few handwritten. Nothing about this nondescript document immediately foretold the dramatic changes it would bring about. Not for Salt Lake City or Utah or for athletic competitions all over the world. And certainly, there was no indication of what it would mean for me.

Yet, as I drove back to the TV station, my Spider-Senses were tingling furiously. I didn't know exactly what I had been given, but my gut told me it was going to be good trouble. Several times I had to remind myself to calm down and focus. But eventually, the curiosity and anticipation got to me. I pulled over, turned off the engine, and picked up the piece of paper lying on the passenger seat. As slowly as I could, I began to digest what the letter actually said:[55]

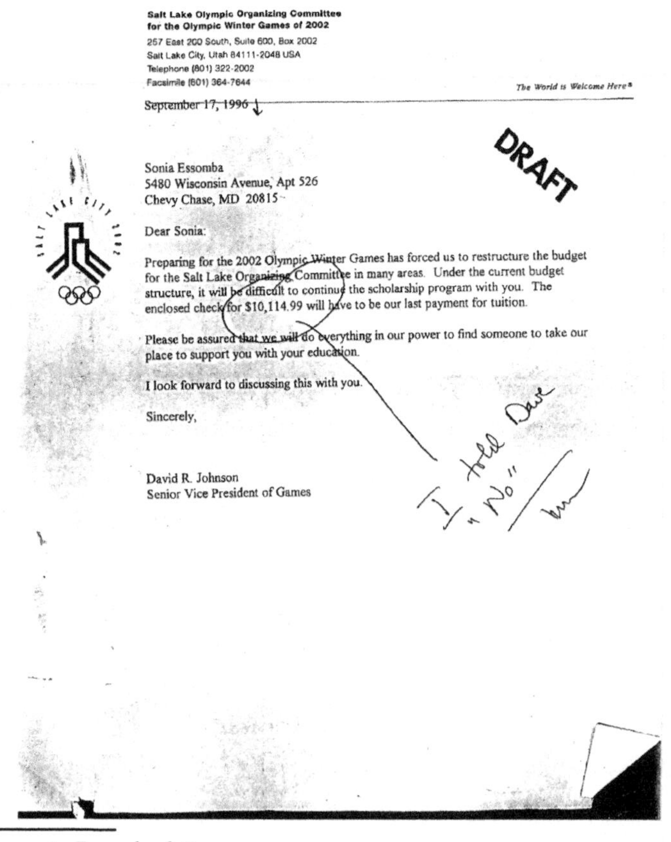

Salt Lake Olympic Organizing Committee for the Olympic Winter Games of 2002
257 East 200 South, Suite 600, Box 2002
Salt Lake City, Utah 84111-2048 USA
Telephone (801) 322-2002
Facsimile (801) 364-7644

The World is Welcome Here

~~September 17, 1996~~

DRAFT

Sonia Essomba
5480 Wisconsin Avenue, Apt 526
Chevy Chase, MD 20815

Dear Sonia:

Preparing for the 2002 Olympic Winter Games has forced us to restructure the budget for the Salt Lake Organizing Committee in many areas. Under the current budget structure, it will be difficult to continue the scholarship program with you. The enclosed check for $10,114.99 will have to be our last payment for tuition.

Please be assured that we will do everything in our power to find someone to take our place to support you with your education.

I look forward to discussing this with you.

Sincerely,

David R. Johnson
Senior Vice President of Games

I told Dave "No"

55. Johnson to Essomba, letter.

This letter was dated September 1996, a little over a year after the International Olympic Committee had awarded the 2002 Winter Games to Salt Lake City. Although not signed, it appeared the letter had been crafted by Dave Johnson, one of the top officials at the Salt Lake (Olympic) Organizing Committee (SLOC). As for the handwritten note on the side of the paper—the one that said, "I told Dave 'No'"—I strongly suspected it had been penned by Tom Welch, the head of SLOC. Welch and Johnson had spent years trying to lure the Olympics to Salt Lake.

But the mystery name in the document belonged to the addressee, Sonia Essomba. My gut told me she was the key here, the reason I had been given the letter. However, I had absolutely no clue who she was. I also wasn't exactly certain how to find out.

When I arrived back at the station, I eagerly showed the letter to one of my bosses. His response was deflating. He looked at it and told me without much enthusiasm to go "check it out." Mildly crestfallen, I returned to my desk and stared at my computer.

It's important to remember the date here: November 1998. The internet was not yet the force it would become. Google had just recently incorporated itself and, being something of a luddite, I certainly had never heard of it. Luckily, just a few days before I got the letter, I had been casually talking with one of the higher-ups at the station. She happened to mention her daughter had been using something called MetaCrawler to do her homework. With no other immediate options at hand, I started to type in all sorts of words and phrases into this search engine.

It didn't go well.

I first checked if there was anyone named Essomba who was part of the IOC. Nope. MetaCrawler showed no connection there. Then I tried typing in Sonia Essomba's name to see if I could figure out exactly who she was. But again, I got no hits and no answers. After any number of attempts and failures, I finally started to type in all sorts of names and words from the letter. Dave Johnson? Nothing useful. Olympic scholarships? Zero hits. Again, remember MetaCrawler's reach was nowhere near what Google's would become.

So, I stopped typing and took another look at the letter, specifically Sonia Essomba's name. Were there clues there I might be missing? As I focused intently on her name, I got unexpected inspiration from my teenage years. I suddenly remembered in high school I had been friends with a girl named Sonia. What's more, her family had been French. With absolutely nothing to lose, I returned to MetaCrawler and typed "Sonia Essomba + France" into the search engine.

Bingo. A twenty-year-old high school memory had borne fruit.

On what looked like the homepage of some sort of private school in France, I got the first useful hint about who Sonia Essomba might be. Relying on the two years of French I'd barely passed in junior high, I translated the information as best I could. It seemed like a Sonia Essomba had briefly attended this French school. Could this be the same person the Olympic letter was addressed to? If so, I wondered if I had stumbled onto something larger. Was there a pattern here, a young girl going to one prestigious school after another?

This was my first solid lead, but now I had to figure out the rest of the puzzle. I took another long look at Sonia Essomba's name, specifically the surname. Was Essomba a French or Spanish name? It had a kind of European feel to it. But my next internet queries yielded little going down this European path. It was only then, when it seemed I had hit another roadblock, that I suddenly remembered something my sources had told me.

Before I got my hands on the Essomba letter, I had been sniffing around Salt Lake's Olympics. Many of the stories done by Utah's press corps about the 2002 Games had been positive in nature. What would the Games mean to our state, how exciting it was that our little city had gotten to host them, etc. And to be fair, I had also done my fair share of these boosterish pieces as well.

But somewhere along the way, I'd started to get tips about the less savory aspects of the Olympics. I was told not everything that glittered was gold. So, bit by bit, I started raising questions about Utah's 2002 Winter Games. And not unlike Bob Woodward, Carl Bernstein, and Ben Bradlee's *Washington Post*, I followed the money. There was a staggering amount of money tied up in the games, and I wanted to know who, if anyone, was profiting.

It was during this time that my sources told me to specifically keep an eye on the IOC members from Africa. According to these sources, some of the African members were a bit "hinky." This was a slangy and shorthand way of letting me know that some of these members might not be on the up and up.

So, just for the hell of it, I returned to MetaCrawler and typed in "Essomba + Africa." My intuitive gamble paid off. I quickly got a hit that led me to a medical research paper. This paper appeared to have been written by someone named Dr. Rene Essomba. My pulse rate began ramping up. The dots were connecting faster now.

Excitedly, I typed: "Dr. Rene Essomba + Africa + Olympics." Finally, MetaCrawler delivered. There, at long last, was a biography of the elusive Dr. Essomba. My eyes quickly scanned his credentials. Curiously, sprinkled in with his impressive medical achievements were a number of sports references. These included participation in various African athletic programs, committees, and foundations. I was clearly getting warmer. And then suddenly, near the end of his bio, I hit pay dirt: "Dr. Rene Essomba, International Olympic Committee Member from Cameroon."

But instead of being elated, I was puzzled. Why hadn't Rene Essomba's name come up at the beginning of my search? After all, I had specifically typed in "Essomba + IOC." Given the way I was wired, I had to know why he hadn't popped up earlier. Had I missed something?

So, one last time, I returned to MetaCrawler. I typed in "Dr. Rene Essomba + Cameroon + Africa + International Olympic Committee." It was this search combination that did the trick. I discovered Dr. Rene Essomba had died just a few months earlier. That's why his name hadn't come up in my earlier searches.

I removed my glasses and took a deep breath. My internet sleuthing had started almost immediately after I got the Essomba letter. It had taken me several hours, but now, finally, the dots had connected. Dr. Rene Essomba had been an IOC member. IOC members decided which cities got to host Olympic Games. And a Sonia Essomba had allegedly gotten scholarship money from Salt Lake's Olympic Committee. Had she received this money because the committee wanted to get his vote? This was the key question I still had to answer.

But after my successful internet discoveries, I tried to temper my expectations and excitement. After all, I still had plenty of work left to do on the story. When I was sure I had all my proverbial ducks lined up in a row, I called Salt Lake's Olympic Committee asking for a comment. To my surprise, SLOC's communications team didn't seem fazed or upset when I told them about the letter. In fact, they even agreed to do a sit-down interview.

Heading into the interview with a SLOC spokesperson, I had two main objectives. First, I needed to confirm Sonia and Rene Essomba were related. I also needed confirmation that some sort of scholarship program had existed. Fortuitously, both objectives were quickly realized.

I was told Sonia Essomba was Rene Essomba's daughter (as I suspected). I was also informed there had been a SLOC scholarship program. But the way this program was explained made me suspicious. The spokesperson said it was essentially for needy students in underdeveloped countries. I had learned long ago that the truth has a sound all its own. To me, this scholarship explanation simply didn't sound like the truth.

After the interview, I probably could have gone back to the station and convinced management to let me run the story. I certainly had enough confirmed to put it on the air. But my intuition was holding me back. It felt like something was still missing.

So, I called Steve Pace.

Pace was well-versed in all Salt Lake Olympic matters, great and small. For years, he had been a highly visible and outspoken critic of the 2002 Games. He was skeptical before they were awarded to Salt Lake and continued speaking out afterward as well. I wanted to interview him because I felt someone (other than me) had to say the letter and the scholarship program might be a problem. This would add greatly to the story's credibility. Luckily, Pace did not disappoint.

I started the interview by showing him the Essomba letter. It took him only a few seconds to grasp its implications. With a hint of indignation, and with the camera rolling, Pace immediately raised the question of whether the payment to Sonia Essomba might be some sort of bribe. He thus became the first person to utter the "B" word.

This, frankly, was why I thought Pace needed to be part of the story. I had already been wondering if the word *bribery* could be attached to the letter, but I was hesitant about bringing up the issue myself. I also didn't think my bosses would be thrilled with me being the one to say it out loud. Fortunately, I didn't have to. Steve Pace did it for me.

Driving back to the station, I felt I had the story nailed down. I had the letter; SLOC had confirmed the two Essombas were related and had acknowledged there had been a scholarship program. Plus, I had the bribery comment from Pace. But even armed with all these solid elements, I still felt some trepidation. I was preparing to break a "Holy Shit" story and was nervous about how my bosses would react. Would they truly understand the significance of what I had uncovered, and would I get the green light to proceed?

Well, whether they understood or not, I quickly got the go-ahead to run the story that night. So, I headed straight to my computer and began to write. Even though this was a somewhat complicated story to tell, the words came out easily. Dad's advice rang in my ears: "Tell them what you're going to tell them. Tell them. And then tell them what you've told them."

Within an hour or so, I had cranked out most of the framework for the script. I deliberately kept the piece as simple as possible. Show viewers the letter, give them SLOC's explanation, and then throw in a quick comment from Pace. I tried not to oversell the story. I hoped the facts would be strong enough to speak for themselves.

At 10:00 p.m. (MST) on November 24, 1998, I sat nervously on our news set. I tried to steady myself before I dropped this Olympic bombshell. But I didn't have much time to process what was about to happen. Before I knew it, the stations' two main anchors read the introduction to my story:

> ANCHORS: Tonight, disturbing new questions about the financial dealings of the Salt Lake Olympic Committee, and that's our top story . . . Salt Lake Olympic organizers have quietly been spending thousands of dollars to pay the college tuition costs of relatives of international Olympic bigwigs. And Chris Vanocur is here with an exclusive investigation.

With that, the anchors turned to me and I began to read what I had written on the teleprompter. The silent mantra echoing in my head was simply, "Don't screw up the intro." At that exact moment, I wasn't thinking about the possible implications of the story. Instead, I was simply concerned about getting through the live intro without stumbling or mumbling. With that embarrassing possibility heavy on my mind, I held up the Essomba letter for the camera and began to read:

> VANOCUR (*Live on Camera*): This is a letter Salt Lake Olympic folks probably didn't want us to get. It raises very serious questions about how Olympic money is being spent and even how Salt Lake got the Olympic bid.

At that point, the story began to air:

> VANOCUR (*Prerecorded Narration*): This confidential letter was drafted in 1996 by a senior Salt Lake Olympic official. It's written to a Sonia Essomba and reads: "Under the current budget structure, it will be difficult to continue the scholarship program with you. The enclosed check for $10,114.99 will have to be our last payment for tuition.

Then came the first comment from SLOC:

> SLOC SPOKESPERSON: I think this is just an example of a program that we had going to help third-world countries and to provide people with educational opportunities.

Following his revelation about the scholarship program, the story continued:

> VANOCUR (*Narration*): But, in fact, Sonia Essomba, this Salt Lake Olympic official later conceded, is not a needy third-world student, but actually the daughter of a prominent surgeon, Rene Essomba, who just happened to be an influential African member of the International Olympic Committee.

The story then showed me at my embarrassingly messy desk. Because we didn't have a lot of video for this story, I narrated this part of it on camera. We had taped it several hours earlier:

> VANOCUR (*Prerecorded on Camera*): In other words, our Olympic committee was paying thousands of dollars to a close relative of somebody who voted on whether or not Salt Lake should get the Olympics.

This was immediately followed by the memorable and crucial soundbite from Steve Pace:

> PACE: This looks like, walks like, and quacks like a bribe being paid out of a publicly-guaranteed organization.

The story continued with my narration:

> VANOCUR (*Narration*): But Olympic officials say this was all private money and that there was nothing improper.
>
> (EXCHANGE BETWEEN VANOCUR AND SLOC SPOKESPERSON)
>
> VANOCUR: Do you think that raises any red flags?
>
> SLOC SPOKESPERSON: Well, these were activities two or three years ago, when this organization was known as a bid committee.
>
> VANOCUR (*Narration*): But look at the date on the letter, September, 1996, more than a year after Salt Lake got the bid. And, according to several highly placed Olympic sources, Sonia Essomba

> was not the only relative of an IOC member to receive large tuition scholarships.

The story then ended with one final comment from SLOC:

> SLOC SPOKESPERSON: There were scholarships that existed from other countries around the world. I do not know what all of their connections were with respect to their national Olympic committees.

All that was left for me now was to read the end of the story live:

> VANOCUR (*Live on Camera*): So tonight, two lingering questions are: Exactly how much has been spent on other people's tuition, and is the practice still ongoing?

After finishing my report, I returned to my desk and sank into my chair. I felt the adrenaline and tension draining from my body. It had been an exceptionally long day. Now, for better or worse, the letter, SLOC's response, and Pace's comment had all been made public. All I wanted was a quiet moment alone to reflect on what had just happened.

I didn't get it.

The phone rang almost immediately. On the other end of the line was Howard Berkes, an extremely talented Salt Lake-based NPR correspondent. He graciously congratulated me on the story. He then asked if I could send him a copy of the script. I told him I would be happy to. Berkes would soon get his version of the story on the air, as did the Associated Press, and the LDS Church-owned newspaper, the *Deseret News*.

In the coming weeks and months, reporters from all over the country and the world would be chasing the story. It had been in my sole possession for only a matter of hours. But that was the rapid nature of the news business. As Dad had said, the never-ending news cycle was an electronic tapeworm constantly demanding to be fed. And thanks to a single piece of paper, an unexpectedly big Olympic meal had just been placed before it.

Chapter Nineteen

"Shitface"

Not long after my November 24 story aired, I reached out to my father. Knowing how much he loved a good story, I called him to let him know what I had uncovered. I also told him there might be more to come. While Dad appreciated the call, I'm not sure he fully understood how quickly the scandal was growing. But to be fair, I'm not sure I did either.

In early December, about two weeks after my initial story, the dam started to burst. SLOC revealed Sonia Essomba wasn't the only one who had gotten money for her education. In fact, SLOC had given out nearly $400,000 dollars in scholarships or financial aid. Many on the receiving end were relatives of IOC members. My sources had been right. What was now unfolding was much bigger than just the Essombas.

Shortly afterward, NPR's Howard Berkes got his own big scoop. He called Marc Hodler, a powerful Swiss member of the IOC, one well-versed in its ethics rules. Hodler told Berkes that SLOC had violated those rules. Hodler would go on to say Salt Lake wasn't the only Olympic city involved in these types of questionable activities.

Before I had time to fully digest what had happened, several major investigations had been launched. SLOC had one, the United States Olympic Committee (USOC) had one, and so did the IOC. Another would soon be added to the list, a probe with potentially more serious consequences.

As these new explosive developments unfolded, I became consumed with the story. Already a workaholic, I knew I had to up my game even more. More late nights, coming in on weekends, whatever it took. I knew instantly this would be the biggest story I would ever break. I was prepared to do whatever it took to chase it.

Unfortunately, this didn't sit well with the woman I was dating. She was the one I'd met at the charity benefit after returning home from Asia. She was less than thrilled I was suddenly going to work on Saturdays and Sundays. Weekends, she said, were supposed to be reserved for her. But much too callously, I decided this story was more important to me than the burgeoning relationship or, for that matter, anything else.

It was about this time that my dad called me back. He had been seeing all the headlines in the news about this seismic Olympic scandal. He asked, "Is this the story you were telling me about? The one involving the Olympics?" I told him it was. He didn't say much, but I sensed he was both impressed and proud. He now realized the magnitude of my scoop. Even though things were crazy busy at the time, I took a moment to savor his call. It felt like a passing of the torch from one reporter to another.

When some but not all of the dust had settled, the wide-ranging scope of the Olympic scandal became much clearer. It was revealed SLOC had paid out more than a million dollars in its efforts to win the 2002 Games. This included not only scholarships but also gifts and cash to IOC members and their relatives. This revelation would eventually cost SLOC's two top leaders their jobs.

The rapidly exploding story even took me and many other reporters to Lausanne, Switzerland, for what was billed as an "extraordinary" meeting of the IOC. The IOC's own internal investigation led to a number of its members either resigning or being expelled. In addition, numerous reforms were implemented to try and clean up the Olympic Games.

I vividly remember sitting in on one of the early sessions of that extraordinary meeting in Lausanne. The IOC announced that, despite the scandal, the 2002 Winter Games would not be moved from Salt Lake. I sat there stunned. I had no idea taking the games away from Utah had even been a possibility. If Salt Lake had lost the Olympics because of my story, I knew I would have been a marked man. In fact, I probably would have been forced to get a job in another state. It's doubtful the good people of Utah would ever have forgiven me for the loss of such a prestigious event.

But the Essomba letter would not be my only big Olympic scoop. During the feeding frenzy of one damaging Olympic development after another, I unexpectedly got a call from one of my A-list sources. This source had just gotten wind of a juicy tidbit, one which would ultimately send the SLOC scandal ricocheting off in a dramatic new direction. The source told me the U.S. Justice Department had begun sniffing around the Olympic scandal.

My reaction was not unlike the one Robert Redford has in the beginning of the movie *All the President's Men*. Redford, as Bob Woodward, is sitting in a courtroom when the Watergate burglars are first brought in. As the burglars tell the judge their names and occupations, Redford leans forward to hear. When the actor playing James McCord says he worked for the CIA, the camera cuts back to Redford on a tight shot. The two words that come out of Redford's astonished mouth are, "Holy shit."[56]

Knowing the feds had subpoena power and the power to indict, I immediately realized the magnitude of this news tip. This investigation, unlike the others, could result in criminal charges and, possibly, even jail time.

So, I quickly called one of my contacts in Washington. This source was wired into whatever was happening at the DOJ. While this D.C. source was skeptical about what I had heard, they agreed to check it out. Not long after, my phone rang. My somewhat surprised source confirmed that, yes, Justice had begun looking into the Olympic matter. It was also considering launching a full-scale investigation. With two excellent sources now confirming, I got the story on the air in time for our afternoon broadcasts.

Eventually, both Tom Welch and Dave Johnson—the two SLOC executives referenced in the Essomba letter—were each charged with fifteen

56. *All the President's Men*.

counts of wrongdoing. These included allegations of fraud, conspiracy, and racketeering.

However, the trial itself was a bit of a shit show. Initially, the case was thrown out by a federal judge in Salt Lake. But it was then reinstated by a federal appeals court in Denver. Finally, in 2003, long after Salt Lake's successful 2002 Games had ended, the same skeptical Salt Lake federal judge dismissed the case for good. Welch and Johnson were cleared of all criminal charges.

But while the judge's ruling was obviously good news for the two former SLOC leaders, the same cannot be said for me. Instinctively, I knew Utah's die-hard Olympic supporters—those who loved hosting the successful 2002 Games and resented the government's prosecution—would be out for blood. And it didn't take long for me to figure out who they would come looking for. They would be coming for the reporter who broke the original story, the one who had shined a harsh negative light on the state.

Unfortunately, my suspicions were soon confirmed.

When I got back to the station, the angry phone messages and emails were waiting. I was indeed being blamed for embarrassing the state and for trying to put Welch and Johnson behind bars. I had heard this kind of chatter for years. But with the charges now having been tossed out for good, I was being tarred and feathered with a vengeance.

All throughout the day and into the night, the hostile reaction continued. Some Utahns were especially venomous. They said I should resign for what I had done. If I wouldn't, they would then urge the station to fire me. Although I didn't actually see it myself, another reporter at the station told me one email referred to me simply as a "shitface." I wondered for a second if they meant shithead and not shitface. But I concluded there really wasn't much of a distinction.

Another email, one I did read, said, "After five years of hearing about the Olympic bid process problems and your investigative reporter being the one that 'broke' the news, I am so glad that a federal judge has vindicated the people that your reporter caused problems [for] during this time... He has caused irreparable damage for our State of Utah and its people, not just for Mr. Johnson and Mr. Welch... I have lost respect with your station and the quality you produce... I hope you take this as constructive criticism and learn how not to do things in the future. Your reporter sort of reminds me of a tenacious animal that won't let go of the neck until their victim dies... I felt sorrow for this whole five-year process and how [your station] was a part of this negative reporting and wouldn't let go of it."

While it may sound a little twisted, I kind of liked being compared to a tenacious animal. That, after all, was my job. I was supposed to be a hard-charging political and investigative reporter. But the rest of the email was troubling. It made me realize some Utahns would never forgive me for the perceived stain my reporting had left on the state.

Normally, after such a grueling and emotionally trying day, I would have gone straight home after the 10:00 p.m. news and had a belt or two. But one of my father's friends was in town and I had already promised to have a late dinner with him.

After a bite and a few drinks at Salt Lake's upscale New Yorker restaurant, I found myself finally starting to unwind. I told my dad's friend about my anguishing day and about some of the backlash against me. Since my dinner companion was also a journalist, I asked him if his work had ever been criticized.

At that point, Pulitzer Prize-winning author David Halberstam just smiled. With a wise and knowing look, David told me that other than being called a traitor by the President of the United States, no, his work had never been criticized. Much to my embarrassment, I had forgotten how the White House had pushed back against his tough reporting in Vietnam.

David then gently reminded me of what I already knew but had forgotten to keep in perspective. He patiently explained how good and aggressive reporting often rubbed powerful people the wrong way. It simply came with the turf. But that didn't mean I should back down or stop doing what I was doing. Even more importantly, it didn't in any way invalidate my reporting or mean that it was wrong.

His comforting words that night didn't silence my Utah critics or make them disappear. But his sound and caring advice was of great comfort after a rough, draining day at work. Because of David Halberstam knowing exactly what to say, I no longer felt like such a shitface.

Chapter Twenty

The Apple and the Tree

"Have you started clearing off your mantle yet?"

This is what one newsroom colleague asked just as the Olympic scandal story reached its zenith. Maybe because I was so intently focused on the story—or because I'm sometimes slow to pick up on things—I simply responded with a blank stare. I had no clue what he was talking about. But, after a few awkward seconds, I asked him what he meant. He just laughed and told me I would need extra space on my mantle for all the reporting awards I was going to win.

Surprisingly, this notion hadn't even occurred to me. Early on in my career, I had been somewhat enamored with awards and entered many journalism contests. Often, I should add, unsuccessfully. But I had been so busy reporting on the Olympic story, winning awards for it hadn't even crossed my mind.

Fortunately, my TV station already had a plan in place. A smart and highly capable news executive was assigned to coordinate our award entries. Eventually, we would enter our Olympic coverage in the country's most prestigious journalism contests. In the summary letter accompanying our award submissions, the station wrote:

> *Hosting the Olympics has been a dream for many people in Utah for more than twenty years. The pursuit of the Winter Games was sanctioned and supported by the top levels of government, Utah's business elite, the mainstream media and the general public. Public*

> *support included financing the bid committee with millions of tax-payer dollars.*
>
> *The drive to host the Olympics also had the approval of the powerful LDS Church, which has its headquarters in Salt Lake City.*
>
> *The principal challenge in covering this story was taking a consistent hard-nosed approach to a popular and generally positive event.*
>
> *The Olympic Games draw worldwide interest. They appeal to our highest ideals.*
>
> *But it is also clear that the modern Olympics are a marriage of corporate and government interests with millions of dollars at stake. Until Vanocur's breakthrough reporting, critical or unfavorable reporting on the Olympics or its principals was considered cynical, and in some circles, unpatriotic.*[57]

Not only did I like this summation, but so, apparently, did the award judges.

The first big honor we received was the George Foster Peabody Award. This is one of the biggest broadcasting journalism awards in the country. The awards are given out annually for excellence in both news and entertainment programming.

After it was announced we had won the Peabody, some newsroom friends took me out for celebratory drinks. We went to a popular Salt Lake saloon named Port O'Call. In true newsroom fashion, we partied well into the evening. Late in the witching hour, a tall and enticing siren walked in. Because we were a fairly large and rather boisterous group at the front of the bar, she made her way over to us.

When she asked why we were all in such a good mood, a close and slightly inebriated friend pointed at me and told her we were celebrating Utah's new Peabody Award winner. He then asked with a bit of a twinkle in his eye, "Would you like to see his Peabody?"

---

57. Award submission.

I can neither confirm nor deny what transpired after that.

In contrast, the actual award ceremony for the Peabody Award was a slightly more dignified affair. The ceremony was held in New York, and the station kindly sent me to accept the honor. My father and stepmother also made the trip back east for the awards luncheon.

In my acceptance speech, I not only thanked my station and my bosses, but I also gave Dad a special shout-out. In explaining to the large audience how a story like this breaks, I said: "It breaks because a long time ago another reporter in this room, one who just happens to share the same last name, taught me clearly and lovingly the distinction between what is right and wrong in this world."

Dad would later proudly brag to his friends that he had been mentioned in my speech.

Another highlight from the awards ceremony came just after the luncheon. As I stood up to leave, I felt a tap on my back. When I turned around, a very friendly and outgoing man congratulated me on the award. He spoke with a fairly heavy accent. He was there because his wife had also been awarded a Peabody. Needless to say, I greatly appreciated Arnold Schwarzenegger's kind words.

As my family and I left the awards ceremony, something rather curious happened. Out of the blue, my stepmother looked at me and said, "You do realize you've peaked way too early." I laughed and didn't give her comment much thought. Only years later did I reflect on what she had said. I eventually concluded she had been right. At age thirty-nine, I had broken the most important story of my career. In the ensuing decade and a half, nothing else would even come close.

As the scandal played out, I was also written about in several magazines and newspapers. I was even profiled in a Japanese paper. Most of these articles were favorable, but a few were not quite so enamored of me or my work.

One of the more balanced pieces was a lengthy story in the *American Journalism Review* (AJR.) It started with a familiar refrain: "Chris Vanocur is no stranger to the famous-father syndrome. Throughout his career as a television journalist, people have often remarked, 'His father is Sander Vanocur.'"

The article went on to explain how the Olympic story helped me emerge from my father's imposing shadow. This was true. While certainly not my dad's equal, I was starting to get national and international recognition. I was even interviewed on ABC's *Nightline*. This small dose of attention was ironically encapsulated in the last line of the AJR story. It mentioned how my dad was now jokingly telling people he was "Chris Vanocur's father."[58]

While I greatly appreciated the AJR piece, it was a local magazine story that truly warmed my heart. In June 2002, *Salt Lake* magazine wrote about the offspring of famous celebrities. Five Utah-based children were profiled; all had followed in their father's footsteps. The magazine even decided to slap my not-so-glamorous mug on the cover.

The first line of the article not only caught my attention, but it has stayed with me for two decades. This lede said simply, "The apple doesn't fall far from the tree." I thought it was a lovely metaphor and an accurate one. I very much saw myself as the fruit descended from a mighty tree.

The *Salt Lake* magazine piece continued by pointing out some similarities in our reporting careers. It noted that my father's aggressive reporting had landed him on Nixon's Enemies List. It then suggested my uncovering of the Olympic scandal had likely landed me on some enemies' lists as well.

But my favorite part of the article was a joint interview with my father. The magazine asked each of us similar questions and then printed the answers side by side.

---

58. Shepard, "An Olympian Scandal."

For example, my father was asked how we were different. Dad told the magazine, tongue in cheek, that I was both rich and organized and that he was not. Then, I was asked how we were alike. I said we both had an unfortunate tendency to tell things as they were.

The last question to my father was especially intriguing. Dad was asked what advice he wished he had given me. He said he didn't have to give me a lot of advice. He then lovingly added that he felt I was smart enough to figure things out on my own.[59]

I smiled wryly when I read this. Some four decades later, my father was apparently no longer worried that there might be "something wrong" with me.

In early 2000, Dad and I also attended the ceremony for the Alfred I. duPont-Columbia University Awards. This prestigious award is considered by some to be broadcasting's equivalent of the Pulitzer Prize. The event was held in New York, and I once again paid tribute to Dad in my acceptance speech.

Afterward, we celebrated at a fancy New York restaurant. We talked about the Olympic story, about politics, and where my career might now be headed. Because we may or may not have consumed more than our fair share of wine, Dad made a quick bathroom pit stop before we left. I waited near the exit. When my father emerged, he walked toward me with a somewhat odd and emotionless expression on his face. Just to be sure everything was okay, I asked him if he was ready to go. He smiled and said, "I'm sorry, sir, I don't believe we've met."

I was momentarily stunned by this remark. Did my own father not recognize me? But after a few baffling seconds, I regained my footing. I told him, "Dad, it's me, Chris." He stared at me for a few seconds while he tried to process this information. Moments later, he snapped back into place. He dismissed his initial confusion by blaming it on the booze. We

59. Lindberg, "Father's Footsteps."

then walked back to the hotel, neither one of us bringing up the awkward episode which had just transpired.

This would be the first time my father forgot who I was.

It would not be the last.

Chapter Twenty-One

A State of Mind

As Dad grew older, his once razor-sharp mind started to slip. Each time I came to visit, he seemed to have deteriorated further. While he still had good days, on others he was quite confused and disoriented.

One time we were watching the Super Bowl at his home in Montecito. He didn't really react to the action on the field, but asked me a half dozen times who was playing. My stepmother told me he had stopped going to movies because he could no longer follow the plots. He would continue to read his big stack of newspapers, but I was no longer sure if he really understood what he was reading.

My stepmother thought Dad often tried to pretend nothing was amiss, especially when he stepped outside the safe confines of home. She also said his intelligence, although waning, was still good enough to fool some people.

My father and I only talked about his dementia one time. It was a short but revealing conversation. It was on one of his more lucid days and he said something that has stayed with me ever since. He told me he couldn't understand why his body was betraying him. I found this fascinating. My father viewed his deteriorating mental capacities not as part of the natural aging process but as a betrayal. He took dementia personally, not unlike the politicians who once attacked him. But this was a much different and more potent foe. Dad's smarts and his fierce determination were, at long last, outmatched.

By the time I started cleaning out his study in early 2016, my father wasn't doing well. I remember we went out to dinner one night at Lucky's restaurant in Montecito. Dad was quiet and content for most of the meal. Just as we were finishing, however, things went off the rails.

My father started asking me a series of very odd and unexpected questions. He wanted to know how I got my job at NBC News and what it was like working there.

I was immediately taken aback at this line of questioning as I had never worked at NBC, and I had no idea how to respond. My stepmom and I exchanged nervous and puzzled glances. Fortunately, she was soon able to get through to him and bring him back to reality. However, he seemed saddened and said little else for the rest of the night.

As we drove back home, it dawned on me what had happened. The circuitry in Dad's brain had once again gotten scrambled. Instead of recognizing me as his son, Dad thought I was someone else. Specifically, he thought I was him. In his mind, I had become Sander Vanocur. That's why he asked about working at NBC. He was now trying to relive and remember his life through me.

As the months went by, Dad's condition worsened. He didn't always know who my stepmom was, and it was hit and miss with me as well. One time, when I mentioned I was going back to Salt Lake, he said he had a son who lived there. On another visit, when I told him I was driving back home, he asked if my daughters were going with me. To the best of my knowledge, I didn't have any children.

During all this, my stepmom heroically carried on. Several years younger than Dad, she took care of him as best she could. But eventually, she had to place him in an assisted care facility. Doing so was very tough on her. I called her the night Dad moved into his new and final home. She was struggling with her decision and emotionally confided in me how much she already missed him. Her husband of more than forty years was no longer by her side.

I would visit Dad there when I could. But our conversations grew shorter and more disjointed. I could tell he wasn't happy though. He thought he had done something wrong and was being punished in some sort of prison. It's heartbreaking for any child to see a parent decline like this, and I certainly was no exception. Knowing how brilliant my father had been made me even sadder.

Some seventy years earlier, my then twenty-one-year-old father had gained national prominence by giving an award-winning speech. But now, the title of that college speech had come back to both haunt and taunt him. Dad's "state of mind" was no longer incisive and impressive. It was simply and sadly gone.

Chapter Twenty-Two

My Wilderness Years

The bigger TV news jobs my father hoped I would get after breaking the Olympic story never materialized. I did land some interviews with national networks—FOX Business and ESPN—but ultimately wasn't hired. While I am pretty good at interviewing others, I grossly underperform in job interviews. I get nervous, intimidated, and quiet. I'm the type of person and employee who tends to impress over weeks, months, and years. But in a short interview session, I underperform. To use the old political saw, I'm more of a workhorse than a show horse.

While I certainly wouldn't have minded a shot at the proverbial "big time," I wasn't crestfallen I didn't get the network gigs. Even though I strongly suspected my father would have liked me to follow in his network footsteps, I made my peace with "only" being a good local reporter. I was fairly well compensated and always lived below my means. This philosophy, plus the low cost of living in Utah, allowed me to live a comfortable but not extravagant lifestyle.

Fortunately, I was self-motivated enough to keep pushing myself. I continued to break significant Utah and national stories, even if they didn't rise to Olympic levels. While I may have grown somewhat comfortable reporting in one place for so long, I never lost my competitive edge. Like Dad, I still viewed other reporters with a certain enmity. Even those I worked with. One day, a station colleague asked me if I would mind if he started doing some political stories too. I told him I would view that as a declaration of war. He thought I was joking. I wasn't.

But over the years, my bosses became less and less impressed I had broken the Olympic story. In fact, it even became something of an albatross. On one occasion, I was sitting in the office of a senior station executive. We had been taking care of some routine business matters when he unexpectedly got up and closed the door. This immediately alarmed me. My intuition told me trouble was on the way.

He proceeded to tell me the Olympic story was viewed negatively by some Utahns. They apparently felt the story had made the state and its residents look bad. He also said there had even been some discussion about whether to let me go because of this. Instead, he said, the station was going to freeze my salary. There would be no more raises for me. I was speechless. I left his office more than a little shaken. I was convinced they were trying to force me out the door.

Fortunately, given the turnstile nature of TV news, it wasn't long before the station got a new owner. My new bosses turned out to be much more appreciative of my work. So, I decided to stay. But perhaps I shouldn't have ignored the flashing warning signals.

It seemed every few years or so, the station was sold to a new company. And after each sale there would be layoffs. I had been spared this fate because I was seen as one of the station's top assets. But eventually, my number came up. In late 2012, my station was again sold to a new owner. Shortly thereafter, significant layoffs occurred. As it was embarrassingly and fully reported in the local papers, I was one of those let go.

A local blogger suggested I might have been terminated because my salary was too high. But I can neither confirm nor deny that. Publicly, the new owners simply referred to the layoffs as a reduction in force.

I thought, perhaps naively, one of the other stations in town would quickly snatch me up. After all, not only had I won the country's top journalism awards, but Salt Lake viewers routinely named me as the top TV reporter in town. But, to my surprise and disappointment, no other local media outlet even bothered to make me an offer.

I was confused by this snub until I talked to one of my smarter sources. When I told him no other Salt Lake station wanted to hire me, he replied, "Did it ever occur to you they don't want your kind of reporting anymore?" I was immediately taken aback. But later, once I had a chance to digest what he said, I realized my source was right.

I had been so consumed by chasing the next big scoop, I'd lost sight of how the TV news world had changed. Increasingly, it seemed stations wanted younger and cheaper reporters. Many of these new hires were expected to do their own photography and editing. Two skills I lacked. There was also increasing pressure to crank out more and more stories. All of these things played against my strengths. I broke the Olympic story because I had good sources, was given the time to do the digging, and had refused to follow the news herd. But all those skills now seemed devalued.

My father once thought he was impervious to the ever-changing headwinds of TV news. He believed, at the end of the day, his talent alone would always protect him. But he had been mistaken. The fact he was an excellent political reporter wasn't enough to sustain and prolong his career. Nor was it enough to save me. I was fifty-three years old and unemployed. I suddenly understood why Dad felt there was nothing sadder in this world than a fifty-year-old local TV reporter.

For the next nine months, I went into a deep funk. It wasn't as bad as the earlier episode when I couldn't get out of bed, but my depression definitely flared up. Always a bit of an introvert, I became something of a recluse. I only left the house to work out or get something to eat. My entire adult life had been wrapped up in reporting. Now, that had been taken from me. Close friends confided they were worried about me. I told them I was fine. But I was worried too.

In the late summer of 2013, I finally landed a TV reporting job in Columbus, Ohio. The pay was good, but less than what I had earned in Utah. My work there was solid and I even managed to break a couple of political stories. I particularly enjoyed covering two of Ohio's higher-profile politicians, Republican Governor John Kasich and Democratic Senator Sherrod Brown. Even though they were on opposite ends of the political spectrum, they were both smart and made for good copy.

Unexpectedly, some of my best work there had to do with the state's heroin crisis. Early on, I covered a meeting at the Ohio Statehouse dealing with this tragic problem. I was shocked when I heard the state's devastating heroin statistics. The skyrocketing numbers of Ohioans using heroin and overdosing were staggering. I immediately sensed heroin was going to become an even bigger problem and story.

After several months and numerous stories on Ohio's drug crisis, Governor Kasich surprised me by praising my opioid reports at a televised public hearing. Later, I was even given an award for my reporting on the issue. I greatly appreciated these acknowledgments and the chance to raise public awareness about this problem.

But eventually, my Ohio assignments brought me less and less fulfillment. For the first time in my career, I started feeling like a bit of a news dinosaur.

One day, I remember being in the company of some other journalists when I saw a breaking news alert on Twitter. Ben Bradlee had died. I sadly mentioned it to these nearby journalists. To my horror, none of my junior compatriots knew who he was. They were simply too young to know what he had meant to the *Washington Post* or to the paper's Watergate coverage.

So, after some two years in Ohio, I decided to hang up my TV reporting spurs for good. I could have stayed perhaps another year and covered the 2016 presidential campaign and election, but I was done. TV news and its internal politics had finally worn me down. Thirty-three years as a reporter were more than enough for one lifetime. The mountains were calling and this not-so-young man decided to head west. It was time to go back home.

My last Ohio story was in November 2015. I was assigned to cover a ceremony honoring a police dog. It was held outside on a cold, rainy, and miserable day. My story was professional but unspectacular. A decade and a half after I broke a huge international story, I was now reporting on canine cops.

My stepmother had been right. I had peaked too early.

Chapter Twenty-Three

Cocaine and Abel

Not long before I said goodbye to Columbus, my family tragically lost another member. One night after work, I was driving to the city's legendary Katzinger's Delicatessen to grab some dinner. But when I was just a few minutes away from the deli, the phone rang. It was my stepmother in California. She was calling with sobering news.

She told me my older brother, Nick, had died. She didn't have too much information but gave me a contact number in Nashville. When I called, I was told Nick had passed away in his sleep. I was immensely sad to hear this but not entirely surprised. Neither was my father. We had both feared things would end this way for Nick. The tragedy of his death was compounded by the fact it could have been averted.

As I hope I've already made abundantly clear, my father was one of those rare individuals who was both highly intelligent and extremely driven. Both qualities helped him to become a highly successful journalist. Without either of them, I doubt he would have achieved what he did. They were both ingrained in his DNA.

But the plot twist here is that Dad passed these traits on to his two sons. Not unlike Solomon, though, he (unwittingly) split them in half. Each of us got one trait and only one. My brother got the smarts. I got the drive.

Nick's interests were broad and brainy. He was into things like competitive bridge, science fiction, and, eventually, personal computing. In school, he took complex math and science classes. His large physics textbook both bewildered and scared me. I couldn't run away fast enough from the advanced things he was studying.

That was the good news. The bad was that he squandered the gift he had been given. Nick just didn't put in the work. He was certainly smart enough to handle the complex subjects he was taking. But he didn't devote enough time to studying them or doing the homework. I still remember when he took some sort of advanced college achievement test in science. It may have been in chemistry. Even though Nick did little to prepare for the exam, he still scored in the higher percentiles. In short, the potential was always there. If not in Dad's chosen journalism profession, then maybe something in the then nascent field of high tech.

But drugs robbed him of his potential.

Near as I can tell, my brother started using around the time he became a U.S. Senate page. This would have made him about sixteen. It was during this time he began to change. He became more distant, started hanging out with a different group of people, and found himself at the center of some troubling incidents. One evening, he wrecked Dad's vintage car in a mysterious crash. Another night, he went to a concert and came home bloodied after an apparent fight. He also seemed to be carrying around an unusually large amount of cash.

Nick's troubling transformation coincided roughly with my family's upheaval in the early seventies. When my parents separated and Mom got sick, it was tough on my brother. I think he felt a bit lonely and neglected. So, he turned to drugs for comfort and companionship. What's long fascinated me, though, is how my brother and I responded so differently to the same sort of familial challenges.

While Nick decided to self-medicate, I chose a different path forward. I was in my early teens when my family was fractured by infidelity and illness. With Dad gone, Mom dying, and Nick on drugs, I also felt adrift. This led me to make an overly dramatic and emotionally charged teenage decision. I decided I could no longer rely on anyone in my family. Therefore, I would go it alone.

This is when I started down the path of becoming a workaholic loner. I used the tremendous drive Dad gave me to blindly forge ahead regardless of whatever obstacles or roadblocks were placed in front of me. I became highly skilled at keeping people and emotions at arm's length.

And it worked. By learning how to fend for and depend on myself, I was able to weather the various family storms around me. But my extreme self-reliance came at a cost. While it helped me navigate the turmoil of my adolescent years, it unknowingly sabotaged my future. As it turns out, living in a fortress of solitude isn't necessarily the healthiest approach to life.

As my therapist would later tell me, I forgot to tear down the emotional wall that had protected me. This "me against the world" attitude that had shielded me in high school became ingrained. I never reverted back to a more normal way of living.

My self-imposed isolation made me leery of trusting anyone. While it may have helped me become a better reporter, it laid siege to my private life. I rarely opened up to the women I dated. My emotions were simply off limits to them. During yet another disintegrating relationship, one of my exes told me she had never felt so alone as when we were dating. Some came to think of me as a Vulcan, someone whose emotions had been removed from their life.

What would only occur to me later is that my brother and I had both become addicts. He had chosen drugs and I had become addicted to work. While it could be argued my addiction was healthier and certainly more financially rewarding, both dependencies left us in similar emotional states. My brother and I were both left largely alone and somewhat broken.

Also, by happenstance, my brother and I both turned to writing to help us sort through our issues. When Nick was several decades into his addiction, he tried his hand at writing a book. I think it was some sort of sprawling novel. He sent copies to my father and to me. But by then, his mind was so fried that his copy was unintelligible. If you think my writing is hard to follow, you should have read his.

Over the years, my brother bounced around the country doing various odd jobs. He even tried his hand at newspaper work at both the *Philadelphia Inquirer* and the *Nashville Tennessean*. I think my father used his contacts to help Nick get these jobs. But, then again, Dad used his contacts to help me get my first TV job.

While Nick had a bit of a knack for writing clever headlines, neither of these newspaper jobs really panned out. But he seemed to like Nashville and it became his final home. He worked for a while at a local restaurant before things finally spiraled out of control. That's when I got the call in 2015.

Because Dad wasn't doing well at the time, I took care of the necessary loose ends. I talked with the police, found a mortuary to handle the cremation, and ordered a copy of the autopsy report. When it arrived weeks later, it showed Nick had died of an overdose of fentanyl. It was not lost on me that while I was busy reporting on Ohio and America's growing drug problem, my own brother had OD'd.

My father's dementia left him confused about exactly what had happened to Nick. When Dad got the heartbreaking news, he repeatedly tried calling my brother on the phone. This was an old reporting habit of his (and mine). If my father had trouble reaching a source, he would simply call and call until he got an answer. But this time no one answered. Even years after Nick's passing, Dad still had trouble processing it. Once, in a moment of confusion and uncertainty, he turned to me and asked, "Nick's dead, right?"

I think my father blamed himself for what had happened. I sensed he felt guilty for not being around more when Nick was growing up. But it's not like my dad didn't try to help. He paid for my brother's therapy and then his rehab. He also supported him financially. But none of it worked. Nick kept using.

While Dad eventually grasped that his oldest son had passed away, he never really seemed to get over it. On one occasion, when my father was a bit more coherent than usual, his overwhelming sadness was plain to see. With a look and tone of despair, he confided to me that Nick had "just pissed his life away." While that may sound harsh, I didn't interpret it that way. To me, it was a raw and honest reflection of Dad's pain. After all, remember what I had told *Salt Lake* magazine about my father and me? We both had an unfortunate tendency to tell things as they were.

Occasionally, I've asked myself if I could have done more to help my brother. But I'm not sure I could have. By the time I reached an age where I might have been of more help, I fear he was already too far gone. I did send him a copy of David Carr's brilliant and chilling memoir *The Night of the Gun*. In it, the *New York Times* reporter and columnist chronicled his own addiction.[60] I hoped the book would show Nick there was a pathway out of dependency. If Carr could do it, so could he. But alas, Nick never responded to or acknowledged my gesture.

In the end, Nick seemed powerless or unwilling to help himself. As one of my smarter and wiser political sources once told me, "Big people make big people decisions." Translated: It's ultimately up to adults to make their own choices in life.

In a somewhat twisted and unexpected sort of way, Nick became kind of a reverse role model for me. When I saw what was happening to him, I made sure I didn't follow him down that same drug-laden path. While I indulged in the usual sort of drinking that went on in high school, I stayed away from the harder drugs he was taking. Once my brother even offered me a free line of cocaine to snort, but I refused. I didn't want to end up in the same bad place he was. Also, as one of my friends later humorously said to me, "Chris, you're too much of a control freak to ever use coke."

My brother's ashes were scattered on Kentucky Lake, not too far from

---

60. Carr, *The Night of the Gun*.

Nashville. This spot was recommended by a kindly local mortician. He assured me the lake was a beautiful and serene place. I hope Nick has finally found peace there.

During Dad's heyday in the 1960s, my family had four members. But a half century later, only two were left. My mother and brother had departed much too soon. Dad and I were now the only ones left.

And soon, it would be just me.

Chapter Twenty-Four

Goodbye

Thirteen has always been a lucky number for me. While some think it brings misfortune, I believe the opposite to be true. I was so convinced of the positive powers of this number that I even wore it on my high school lacrosse jersey.

But that all changed on September 13, 2019. Or, to be more specific, Friday the thirteenth.

That afternoon I had been attending a memorial service for Tom Nissalke. He was the former coach of the Utah Jazz basketball team, the one professional sports franchise I have long been passionate about. I had gotten to know Tom through his daughter, Holly, who was a close friend.

After the service ended, I left the church and began walking to my car. Literally seconds after I stepped outside, my phone rang. It was my stepmother calling. It wasn't just bad news; it was tragic.

She told me my ninety-one-year-old father had come down with pneumonia and was being moved to hospice. As I stood there in the church parking lot listening to her, I couldn't help but note the timing. Just as I was leaving a memorial service for a friend's father, I got a call that my own dad was dying.

I quickly made arrangements to fly to Santa Barbara that evening. Delta Air Lines was especially accommodating, giving me a bereavement fare and even bumping me up to first class. As odd as it may sound, I wrote most of my father's obituary on the flight to California. Another friend who had recently lost her father had given me the idea. She said it was easier and less emotional to do it before the loved one was actually gone. She was right.

When I reached Montecito late that night, my stepmother and I greeted each other with a long, heartfelt hug. We both realized the terrible circumstances that had brought us together. The end was near.

Most of the next seventy-two hours remain a grief-stricken blur.

My stepfamily and I spent the weekend taking turns at Dad's bedside. By that point, he was incapacitated. He had a fairly high fever and his breathing was labored. He couldn't talk and we had no idea if he could hear or understand us.

The most emotional part of the weekend came when my stepmother and I were sitting opposite each other next to Dad's bed. She was holding his left hand; I held his right. At one point, Dad started squeezing our hands as hard as he could. He tried to lean forward to speak, but we couldn't comprehend what he was trying to say. It was as if he was using all his remaining energy and determination to try and stave off death.

I was a mess. Tears were streaming down my face. I simply couldn't deal with the enormity of losing someone who had meant so much to me. At one point, I happened to look over at my stepmother. I marveled at how she was keeping it together. She was concerned yet calm. Looking back at this highly charged episode now, I think this was my father's finale.

Late on the evening of Monday, September 16, my stepmother got the call. Dad had passed away. As our family gathered in the living room to let the news sink in, my stepmother and I reversed our earlier roles from the hospice. She rightfully looked stunned and wondered out loud what she was going to do now that he was gone.

On the other hand, I became hyperrational. I started mentally checking off all the things that had to be done. Even though our family was privately grieving, a public statement would have to be prepared and released. Rightly or wrongly, I felt my father's legacy was now in my hands. So, I channeled the inner drive Dad had bequeathed me and immediately went to work.

First, I posted an announcement on Twitter about his passing. I hashtagged the various media outlets he had worked for and others I thought might be interested. Because it was approaching midnight on the East Coast, I thought his death wouldn't attract much attention that night. But come the next day, I knew there would be substantial interest. To that end, I left phone messages for the Associated Press, the *New York Times*, and the *Washington Post*.

I spent much of Tuesday talking with various reporters and close friends of the family. I also added a few final edits to the obituary I had written on the plane. Oddly, I found these sorrowful duties to be welcome diversions. They helped distract me from my enormous grief.

The *New York Times* would soon run a lengthy and comprehensive article about my father's passing. My family was quite appreciative of the significant space the paper devoted to him and his life. The *Times* obit talked about my dad's substantial role in the early days of TV news. It mentioned his coverage of the Kennedys, Vietnam, and his "fraught relationship" with Nixon. As I read what the *Times* had written, I was reminded that Dad had often told me what an honor it was for him to have worked there.

The *Washington Post* was also quite generous with its coverage. Its article covered much of the same ground as the *Times*, but also included a link to my father's interview with Dr. Martin Luther King Jr. Given how strongly my father felt about civil rights, I think Dad would have liked that.

The TV news networks also reported my father's passing but much more briefly. Even though Dad had risen to fame on television, it was the newspapers that most extensively covered his death. This irony was not lost on my family or me.

Finally, there was the obituary I wrote for the Santa Barbara newspapers. The first section was not much different than what ran in the *Times* and the *Post*. But I also added a more personal touch at the end:

> *On one occasion, his son Christopher had the honor of introducing his father before a speaking engagement. He asked his dad what he should say. Vanocur Sr. told him, "Son, use lots of adjectives."*
>
> *With that in mind, here are some adjectives which best describe Sander Vanocur: brilliant, courageous, eloquent, witty, complex, charismatic, driven, passionate, historic, and loving.*

I hoped my father would have approved.

Interestingly Dad had come up with his own epitaph years before. Near the end of his interview with the Freedom Forum, he was asked what he would like people to know about Sander Vanocur. He answered, "I'd like people to remember Sander Vanocur as a hardworking journalist who tried to do the right thing and, upon several occasions, did."

As mentioned often here, Dad certainly had a way with words.

When I was done talking with all the media outlets, calling Dad's friends, and submitting his obituary to the local papers, I took a moment for myself. I stepped outside to collect my thoughts. I took a seat in the backyard and looked out over the mountains and the ocean.

And then I lost it. Big time.

After decades of being an emotionless Vulcan and hiding my feelings, I finally let my guard down. The tears started as a trickle but soon became uncontrollable. My body shook with heaving sobs. The loss I felt was almost unbearable. As one of my friends would later observe, my love for my father was palpable.

Eventually, though, my tears dried. Sitting outside with the magnificent West Coast vista in front of me, I took a long look at the water on the horizon. I knew Dad's ashes would soon be scattered in the Pacific. Whenever I travel on or over this ocean now, I sense he watches over me still.

As noted earlier, when Martin Luther King Jr. was killed, my father paraphrased what John O' Hara had said about the passing of George Gershwin: "I didn't want to believe he was dead. I still don't."

I didn't want to believe my father was dead. I still don't.

EPILOGUE

THERE IS ONE final document from Dad's study to be shared. It's a letter written to my father by a longtime fan. It's dated February 23, 1991. It strongly urged him to write a memoir, one focusing on the stories he covered and the remarkable people who shaped his life. The letter ended by reminding my father this would be a very "worthwhile endeavor." It was signed with the heartfelt sentiment, "Love, Chris."

The letter was written by me. I found it in a rather formally named file, "Chris Book Proposal."

I only vaguely remembered having sent this letter and was surprised he'd held on to it for two and a half decades. But I didn't just urge my father to write a memoir; I also offered to help. I told him I would be happy to record a series of interviews with him and then organize them into a rough framework for the book. He could then finish writing it himself. Interestingly, that framework would not have been all that different from what I've written here.

My father would have been sixty-three years old at the time, just about the age I am now. It would have been a perfect time for Dad to craft his memoir. His network news career was winding down and he had plenty of time to write. Not only that but his mind would still have been sharp enough and his memory largely intact. As an added bonus, he could have written it in his picturesque Montecito study.

But my father politely rejected my offer. He said (kindly) I should instead concentrate on writing my own book.

Every now and then, I would bring up the matter again. Sometimes Dad would say he simply didn't think his life was that interesting. On other occasions, he would decline by saying it was poor form to talk about oneself too much. But none of these explanations struck me as adequate or entirely truthful.

In reality, Dad's self-professed lack of organizational skills was an obstacle. Also, he may have lacked the necessary patience and discipline to write his story. His mind was wired to be active, curious, and restless. The idea of sitting down for hours/days/months to write was probably not very appealing to him. He was fond of repeating that old quote about writing, "You simply sit down at the typewriter, open your veins, and bleed."

My suspicions about my father's hesitancy or inability to write a memoir were reinforced by what I found in his study. There were several high-profile book proposals stashed away in his files. It appeared he may have even gotten some lucrative advances to write them. But he never did. So, I have done it for him. I have written his life's story. It is my final gift to him.

Not that any of it came easily. I've bled more than a little onto my keyboard. But after any number of false starts and narratives, I finally discovered the way forward. It was only when I combined my father's life with mine that everything came together. Our stories were so intertwined, it seemed only natural to tell them together. Oddly, the book I wanted my father to write and the one he urged me to write turned out to be more or less the same.

I've done my best to follow Dad's admonition: "Tell them what you're going to tell them. Tell them. And then tell them what you've told them."

The story I've tried to tell was about a great yet imperfect man. I've highlighted the many shining moments of his career and the history-making stories and people he covered. But I've also shared his professional lows. Nixon caused the worst; Dad's occasional self-destructive tendencies caused some others.

And even though it made me uncomfortable to do so, I also provided a glimpse into Dad's personal life. There were his two marriages and his dalliances. His two children are also mentioned, as are the high and lows each brought him. I don't think my father would have liked me sharing all these confidential tales, but he was always proud and supportive of my work. I suspect he would have ultimately understood why I included some family secrets. After all, they were part of the story and he always taught me to pursue my stories with great vigor.

I now close as I began, by referencing Russell Baker. In his own memoir, Baker wrote about the power of words to take us places. Words took Baker and my father from modest beginnings to the very top of their professions. Words also took Dad to assignments all over the country and world. He saw racism in the deep South and American imperialism gone awry in Southeast Asia.

When I began writing this book, though, I didn't fully understand Baker's point. I assumed he was just talking about the power of words to take us to different lands or maybe professional heights. But, in my case, the power of words took me not to a place or a prominent job but to a person. They brought me back to my father. The words I found in Dad's study—in his scripts, articles, speeches, and letters—brought him and his brilliance back to life. Even more importantly, they also brought him closer to me.

Dad often said if you make your story compelling enough, the audience will be drawn to it as well. This is ultimately why I wrote Dad's memoir for him. What I found in my father's study was absolutely fascinating to me. I hoped and suspected it might be to others as well.

But I also had another reason for writing this book. I wanted a final chance to say goodbye.

Dad's declining mental state prevented us from having a more complete ending. I never got to bid him a proper farewell or adequately thank him for all he had done. Not for the education he had given me, nor for helping shepherd me through my life and career. Most painstakingly, I never got a final chance to thank my father for the unconditional love he gave me. Although it was sometimes awkwardly expressed between us, our affection and devotion to each other was real and everlasting.

I would have also thanked my father for trusting me with his papers. For many years, for whatever reasons, he resisted organizing them himself or letting anyone else do it. But he granted me access to his study and allowed me to dive deep into the most important moments of his life. And, in so doing, he gave me an unexpected gift. He helped me find my voice.

As mentioned before, the arc of my TV career was stunted because my narration wasn't very good. Although I worked endlessly at it, my on-air delivery never sounded natural. But switching from TV to print changed everything. Writing this book helped me discover a more honest and liberating voice. This new voice permitted me to share both fond and hard truths about my father, about me, and about our lives together. While my voice never rang true on TV, in print it sounded just fine.

Because I still don't want to believe my father is gone, I will close with a final treasured moment between us.

Late one afternoon, when I had almost finished organizing his papers, my father made a surprise appearance in his study. He wandered in quietly and went straight to his desk in the opposite corner of the room. I watched him surreptitiously as I went about my work. Dad haltingly picked up a random piece of paper for closer inspection. While he didn't explain what he was doing, I quickly figured it out. He had come to try and help. Although most of his legendary drive had long since deserted him, he still wanted to be there to help with the packing up of his life.

But I could tell my father was struggling. He stared at the paper for several minutes before finally giving up. While I appreciated the effort, I think it was all simply too much for him. His eyesight and comprehension were no longer up to the task.

Dad sat there silently for a few minutes before getting up and slowly making his way toward the exit. Since there wasn't much left to be done, I told him I would walk back to the house with him.

As we carefully made our way down the steep driveway, I suddenly felt the need to reach out to him, to let my father know how much I admired and loved him. So, in a rare moment of spontaneity and openness, I said, "You know, Dad, you really had a remarkable life."

He stopped and turned to me. Because of his diminished state, I'm not sure he really understood the affectionate compliment I had just given him. Instead, with a look of childlike wonder and amazement, he asked innocently, "I did?"

Yes, Dad, you did.

ACKNOWLEDGMENTS

WHEN IT CAME to writing this book—and my life in general—I am grateful for the people I have found. With that in mind, let me give heartfelt thanks to those who have been of immeasurable help.

Donna Rifkind is a longtime friend and writing mentor. Her advice during this project has been invaluable. I heartily recommend her book, *The Sun and Her Stars.*

I've known Bruce Baird for some forty years. He was the first person to read the completed manuscript and his encouragement convinced me to publish this book.

Muffy Mead-Ferro wisely suggested I follow the self-publishing route. She is the author of the clever and entertaining *Confessions of a Slacker Mom.*

Bill Lord was once my TV boss and is now a valued friend. He helped guide me through the labyrinth of the self-publishing world. His terrific book, *50 Years After Vietnam,* provided a valuable blueprint.

Editor Debra Ginsberg provided much needed guidance with the structure and themes of the book, as well as helping me come up with the title.

Copy editor Stephanie Slagle gave me another valuable set of eyes and helped shepherd me towards publication.

The cover design and formatting was done capably and reliably by Clark Kenyon.

Mikael Short valiantly proofed and polished the manuscript. She is both a former colleague and a friend.

I also wanted to express my gratitude to the Freedom Forum and the John F. Kennedy Presidential Library and Museum. They were kind enough to interview my father and to share the interview transcripts with him.

Additionally, my thanks to the *Salt Lake City Weekly*, *Vamoose Utah*, and Copperfield Publishing. They have all been loyal supporters of my writing and I am indebted to them.

I am also indebted to the college textbook, *Broadcast News: Writing, Reporting, and Producing*. It proved to be a valuable resource when writing about my Olympic reporting.

My stepmother, Virginia Vanocur, also played a key role. She was the one who asked me to organize Dad's study and that planted the seed for this book. My stepsister, Daphne, has provided valuable support over the years as well.

Others who have helped me immeasurably along the way are: Vasilios Priskos, Bianca, Jennifer Bolton, the always adventurous Dr. Adams, and my dear friend "T."

Finally, I must express my heartfelt gratitude to Blake and Ryan. Their unconditional and unknowing friendship and support have meant the world to me.

BIBLIOGRAPHY

1. Baker, Russell. *The Good Times.* William Morrow and Company, Inc., 1989.
2. "Vanocur Wins First in 42nd Annual Kirk Oratorial Contest." *Daily Northwestern,* February 16, 1949.
3. "Vanocur Wins Northern Speech Meet." *Daily Northwestern,* May 10, 1949.
4. Vanocur, Sander. "A State of Mind." Speech, Northwestern University, 1949.
5. Haffner, Sebastian. "World Power To-morrow." *Sunday Observer,* February 11, 1951.
6. Vanocur, Sander. "Two World Powers." *Sunday Observer,* February 18, 1951.
7. *The Paper Chase.* United States: Twentieth-Century Fox, 1973.
8. Burritt, Richard D. Letter from Richard D. Burritt to Sander Vanocur. New York, NY, September 13, 1957.
9. Vanocur, Sander. "1,000 Celebrate Wiener-Beer Day." *New York Times,* May 20, 1957.
10. Talese, Gay. *The Kingdom and the Power: Behind the Scenes at The New York Times: The Institution That Influences the World.* Cleveland: World Publishing, 1962.
11. NBC Souvenir Booklet, 1960s.
12. Frank, Reuven. *Out of Thin Air: The Brief Wonderful Life of Network News.* Simon & Schuster, 1991.

13. Vanocur, Sander. Transcript of Interview with Freedom Forum.
14. Vanocur, Sander. "Humphrey vs. Kennedy: High Stakes in Wisconsin." *The Reporter Magazine*, March 17, 1960.
15. Vanocur, Sander. "Debates have come a long way since 1960." Boston.com. October 3, 2000.
16. Vanocur, Sander and Richard Nixon. Transcript of 1960 Presidential Debate, Kennedy vs. Nixon.
17. Nixon, Richard. *Six Crises*. Doubleday, 1962.
18. Kennedy, John F. Inscription on JFK's Debate Notes to Sander Vanocur. February 1961.
19. Vanocur, Sander. "The Kennedy Sixties." 1983.
20. Vanocur, Sander. "Kennedy's Voyage of Discovery." *Harper's Magazine*, April 1964.
21. Zelizer, Barbie. *Covering the Body: The Kennedy Assassination, the Media and the Shaping of Collective Memory*. University of Chicago Press, 1993.
22. Salinger, Pierre and Sander Vanocur. *A Tribute to John F. Kennedy*. Encyclopædia Britannica, 1964.
23. Vanocur, Sander. Transcript of Interview with Freedom Forum.
24. Franklin, Andrew K. "King in 1967: My Dream Has 'Turned into a Nightmare.'" NBCNews.com. NBCUniversal News Group, August 27, 2013.
25. Vanocur, Sander. "After Civil Rights: Black Power." NBC News, June 11, 1967.
26. King Jr., Martin Luther. "I've Been to the Mountaintop." Speech, Memphis, TN: Mason Temple, April 3, 1968.
27. Cowan, Reed. Interview with *QSaltLake Magazine*. 2009.

28. Buttars, Chris. Interview with Reed Cowan for *8: The Mormon Proposition*. 2009.
29. Seinfeld, Jerry. *Seinfeld*. "The Outing." 1993.
30. *Dear America: Letters Home from Vietnam*. United States: HBO, 1988.
31. Vandiver, Frank. E. *Shadows of Vietnam: Lyndon Johnson's Wars*. Texas A&M University Press, 1997.
32. Vanocur, Sander. Speech, Louisiana State University, Baton Rouge.
33. Vanocur, Sander. "How the Media Massaged Me." *Esquire* Magazine, January 1972.
34. Greene, Graham. *The Quiet American*. United Kingdom: William Heinemann London, 1955.
35. Kennedy, John F. and Sander Vanocur. Transcript of Interview for JFK Oral History Collection. John F. Kennedy Presidential Library and Museum, 1973.
36. Kennedy, Robert F. Letter from RFK to Sander Vanocur. November 16, 1964.
37. Newspaper clip. *The Washington Post*, September 4, 1966.
38. Margolick, David. "Robert F. Kennedy's Final Flight: The Storied Journey of the Ride from California to New York." *The Washington Post*, June 3, 2018.
39. Kennedy, Ethel. Handwritten Letter from Ethel Kennedy to Sander Vanocur. Christmas 1968.
40. Freund, Betsy. "A Very Confused Man." *Harper's Magazine*, December 1971.
41. Dean, John. White House Memo. 1971.
42. MacNeil, Robert. Interview for *Santa Barbara News-Press*. 1971.

43. Haldeman, H.R. White House Memo. November 17, 1969.

44. Huntsman Sr., Jon M. White House Memo. September 23, 1971.

45. Whitehead, Clay. White House Memo. November 24, 1971.

46. Thomasson, Dan."Vanocur's Fat Salary Angers White House." *Washington Daily News*. November 26, 1971.

47. Cartoon. *Washington Daily News*, November 29, 1971.

48. *Oxford Languages* Dictionary. "Yippie."

49. Bachrach, Judy. "Election show has 2 pluses: Vanocur, brevity." *Baltimore Sun*, March 8, 1972.

50. Higby, Lawrence. White House Memo. June 10, 1972.

51. Brown, Les. "Files of Nixon White House Show Bid to Control Public Broadcasting." *New York Times*, February 24, 1979.

52. Miller, Arthur. *Death of a Salesman*. New York: Viking Press, 1949.

53. Bradlee, Ben. Inscription in *A Good Life* for Chris Vanocur.

54. Vanocur, Sander. "Can Democracy Survive the Mass Media." Speech.

55. Johnson, David R. Letter from David R. Johnson to Sonia Essomba. Salt Lake City, UT, September 7, 1996.

56. *All the President's Men*. United States: Warner Bros., 1976.

57. Award submission letter.

58. Shepard, Alicia C. "An Olympian Scandal." *American Journalism Review*, April 1999.

59. Lindberg, Kelley J.P. "Father's Footsteps." *Salt Lake Magazine*, June 2002.

60. Carr, David. *The Night of the Gun: A Reporter Investigates the Darkest Story of His Life. His Own*. Simon & Schuster, 2009.

ABOUT THE AUTHOR

Chris Vanocur has won the two most prestigious awards in TV news broadcasting: the Alfred I. duPont-Columbia University Award and the George Foster Peabody Award. He received these after uncovering the worldwide scandal surrounding Salt Lake's 2002 Olympic Games. He has also written several award-winning articles about politics, as well as chronicling his travels around America and overseas. He can be found on Twitter, Instagram, and TikTok either under his name or @NewsVulcan. (Picture courtesy of Donny Sobnosky.)